Instructor's Manual to Accompany

CONNECTIONS
A Multicultural Reader for Writers

Lorraine Lordi
Judith Stanford

Rivier College

Mayfield Publishing Company
Mountain View, California
LONDON • TORONTO

International Standard Book Number: 1-55934-197-1

Manufactured in the United States of America

Mayfield Publishing Company
1240 Villa Street
Mountain View, California 94041

CONTENTS

CONNECTIONS: TEACHING ACROSS CULTURES

Suggestions in this guide are intended to open possibilities, not to dictate absolute answers or to insist that certain patterns or processes must be followed as you teach using *Connections*. Both in the text and in this guide, we've tried to include writing topics and suggestions for discussions that will work with diverse teaching and learning styles. We would be most interested to hear from you. Let us know what has worked well for you and your students and what has not. Most of all, we would appreciate your sending suggestions for innovative teaching strategies that we might include in the next edition of this guide.

STRATEGIES FOR MAKING CONNECTIONS

In any classroom, but most certainly within a classroom where the subject matter addresses diversity in a lively and often controversial way, instructors are faced with complex, often frustrating tasks. These include:

- promoting lively discussion that includes all students and does not degenerate into petty bickering between a few outspoken individuals
- encouraging honest, yet fair-minded writing that takes risks and also indicates an ability to communicate clearly and logically
- developing innovative ways of assessing students' writing in order to encourage both achievement of high standards and growth of self-confidence

Creating a Community in the Classroom

Because students will be sharing their ideas (and probably their writing) with each other, we believe it is essential for them to develop a sense of trust as early in the semester as possible. Developing trust begins with breaking down the barriers and challenging the easy assumptions that exist before people get to know one another as individuals. You may want to consider these possibilities:

1

- Learning your students' names as quickly as possible and using their names whenever you speak to them—a painless way to help them learn each others' names. (One way to learn names early in the semester is to arrive at the classroom several minutes before class begins and to ask each student's name as he or she enters. Then jot down a brief descriptive phrase next to the student's name on the roster. In addition, once the student has chosen a seat, write his or her name on a diagram of the room's chairs. Then ask students to take the same seats for the next few classes.)

- Arranging the chairs so that students can look at each other as they speak, rather than funneling all responses through the instructor (a circle or semi-circle of desk-chairs, for example, or standard chairs grouped around a seminar table).

- Taking a few minutes of the first class to do a get-acquainted exercise. This can be very simple: Ask each student to jot down three statements describing him- or herself and then have students give their names and read their statements (you may want to prepare your own three statements, as well).

   Another, more time-consuming, but effective, exercise asks students to prepare to introduce any of their fellow classmates to the instructor. After giving these instructions, the instructor leaves the room and the students spend fifteen or twenty minutes learning each others' names. When the instructor returns, students return to their seats, and then each is asked to introduce the student sitting to his or her left.

Developing an Interactive Classroom

For a course that teaches reading, writing, and critical thinking, we believe an interactive structure works more effectively than does a traditional, lecture-dominated structure. In the interactive classroom, students and instructor work together. The instructor does much more than simply prepare a lecture and deliver information to students. Students do much more than read assignments, listen to lectures, and deliver unprocessed information back to the instructor through exams and papers.

In the interactive classroom students take responsibility for their own learning while the instructor provides whatever help and encouragement they need to accomplish this task. Some strategies that encourage interactive learning include the following.

Divide a large class into small groups for discussion or for work on writing projects. Often, students who are uncomfortable speaking or asking questions in a large class situation are more at ease when they work in groups of three to five. Consider the following issues:

- *Should students choose their own groups or should the instructor assign groups?* We like to vary the approach, sometimes asking students to form their own group and at other times assigning groups to insure a variety of voices.

- *Should instructors participate in groups or stay away?* Opinion varies greatly among the proponents of group work. Most believe that instructors should interfere very little. Some believe that the instructor should leave the room entirely while groups meet. Another approach calls for the instructor to sit alone for the first few minutes, reading or writing and not looking at students. After the groups have started discussion, the instructor moves around from group to group, mostly listening, but occasionally responding to a question or making a comment.

- *Should groups always or nearly always work toward or reach consensus?* We think it's important to stress that the point of much group work is to discover multiple possibilities. Certainly students should be encouraged to think critically about each other's ideas, but it's not always necessary or desirable that a group arrive at a single, neatly planned response.

- *How should small group discussions be structured?* While there are many ways to structure small groups, here's one possibility:

    Ask students to give their names before they speak for the first time and encourage them to address each other by name.

    Ask one student volunteer to be the group recorder—to take notes and to speak for the group if the class reconvenes as a whole.

Encourage students to be sensitive to the dynamics of the group; make each responsible for speaking, yet not dominating, and for seeking out the opinions of those who may not as readily volunteer their ideas.

Conduct a listening workshop. To stress the importance of listening as a learning device, consider conducting a workshop that encourages students to think about listening skills. This is a good way, early in the semester, for an instructor to open the door for strong, productive classroom conversation. A listening workshop may take between 20 and 30 minutes and follows these steps:

- Explain the process of asking open-ended questions. To begin with, suggest that students ask only questions that begin with the following words: *what, where, when, who,* and *how.* (The word *why* tends to set up defensive situations.)

- Based on the instructions above, invite students to interview you for two minutes (take one question from as many different students as possible during this time).

- After the time is up, ask students to summarize what they have heard and invite several volunteers to read their summaries aloud.

- Discuss the differences and similarities in these summaries, stressing strengths rather than weaknesses.

- Now students should be ready to engage in listening to one another. Ask each student to pair up with someone he or she doesn't know. After the pair decides who will "speak" first and who will "listen," the initial "listener" should ask a general, nonthreatening question such as "What is your favorite season?"

- The "speaker" answers, and as soon as he or she is finished, the "listener" begins to ask appropriate questions, based on the guidelines given in the first suggestion in this list. Continue for two minutes.

- When the time is up, the "listener" then summarizes for the "speaker" what he or she said.

- The "speaker" then briefly explains his or her response to this summary.

- Now the partners switch roles, and the new "speaker" answers the questions, following the steps of the process as just described.

Be aware of the dynamics of full class discussions.

- Recognize that the arrangement of chairs can help or hinder free exchange of ideas. Arranging chairs in a circle or semi-circle—so that students can see each other as they speak—usually works best.

- Understand that students often choose to sit in the same seats at each class and that "silent ghettos" can develop—areas of the classroom from which no voices are heard. You may find that you can sometimes break the silence barrier by choosing to sit or stand in that area of the classroom and then speaking directly to students who are sitting there. If anyone makes eye contact with you, direct your next query or "long pause" toward him or her.

- Recognize that some students may dominate discussion. To allow students who may be shy or who may think more cautiously than others the time to speak, consider watching the clock and, at some class meetings, announcing halfway through the session that you appreciate the hard work and thoughtful observations made by those who have already commented. Then encourage these hard-working talkers to sit back and enjoy listening for the rest of the class period (or for the next ten or twenty minutes or whatever seems right) while those who have not yet spoken offer their ideas. Sometimes you may have to wait many seconds before one of the quieter students volunteers, but once one has spoken, the floodgates open. (This strategy works best if the discussion has started with warm-up writing. Then everyone has some thoughts committed to paper. Reluctant speakers may be willing to read what they have written as a way to begin their participation.)

- Understand that gender issues can affect classroom participation. Research suggests that, contrary to popular belief, men tend to dominate discussions and to interrupt more often than women do. In addition, discussion often follows "gender runs." If a man speaks first, then other men are likely to follow. When a woman does break into the conversation, others usually follow her. If you notice a gender run going on too long, consider interrupting and directing the discussion to someone of the opposite sex. Watch students carefully and choose someone who looks like he or she is waiting with something to say.

- Understand that cultural differences may affect willingness to participate in class discussion. For instance, some silent students may come from cultures where teachers do all the talking and where it is considered extremely rude to challenge or question a statement made by an authority figure. In addition, students whose first language is not English may fear that others will laugh at or be impatient with their hesitant or less-than-grammatically perfect speech. You may want to meet privately with hese students to encourage them to speak, yet also to let them know that you respect their concerns. Consider suggesting that they arrive at class with a prepared observation or comment on the assigned reading. Let them know that you will invite them to offer their prepared observation before you call on other students. This strategy gets them speaking in class yet also alleviates the pressure and anxiety of not being able to "find the right words" or of not yet having developed the ability to jump into the middle of a lively discussion.

Require at least one office conference for each student. Seeing students on a one-to-one basis, as early in the semester as possible, provides them with an opportunity to discuss any concerns they may have about the class. In addition, the early visit shows them the way to your office, lets them know that you are available, and encourages them to return with any questions or observations they may have about the assigned reading and writing.

WRITING TO MAKE CONNECTIONS

In addition to interactive discussion, varied approaches to writing lead to a classroom climate that promotes trust, mutual respect, and intellectual as well as personal growth. While none of the following suggestions replaces the formal paper, written out of class, they encourage students to see writing as a process that takes many forms and has many different purposes.

Warm-up Writings

Ask for a few minutes of brainstorming on paper to get students writing early and often. Encourage them to use what they have written to initiate discussions (or to restart a discussion that has ground to a halt or is bogged down in repetitive responses). Usually if you ask them to gather their thoughts through jotting down responses to a topic or a series of topics, students will more readily participate in discussions. Several things happen with such warm-ups: Students discover ideas they didn't know they had; they are forced to really think about the discussion subjects, rather than turning their brains to "rest and recuperate" mode when you ask for responses; and, finally, those students who think things through slowly and carefully, rather than responding immediately, are given time to ponder and are not left behind while those who speak more readily race from one idea to the next.

The prereading questions that precede each selection provide possible topics for warm-up writings. In addition, the photographs and preview quotations that introduce each thematic section offer opportunities for students to ponder and predict the questions, topics, motifs, issues, and conflicts to be addressed in the selections that follow.

Journals

If you plan to have students keep journals during the semester, Section One introduces journals and provides an opportunity for you to describe what you expect. How many entries do you want students to write each week? Will you specify a length for each entry? Should the entries be carefully written, revised, and edited? Or are the journals to be a place where students can explore ideas, free from the restraints of formal writing?

Journal entries can be the most important writing the students do during the semester, and, in addition, they provide the instructor with a fine opportunity to encourage and reward risk taking. Consider urging students to see their journals as a place to try out ideas and to explore responses to both the selections they read and class discussions.

To provide some guidelines, you might ask students to write at least two entries each week that, together, would total approximately 250 words. At least one entry per week would respond to the selections assigned for reading and discussion during that week. The other entry might explain new thoughts about works read earlier or might comment on issues raised during class discussion. Using these guidelines, then, students would receive full credit as long as they submitted the amount of writing required.

Like warm-up writings, journal entries may be used as a way to get discussion started, either by inviting volunteers to read entries they may have written on a specific selection or by asking students to work in small groups, reading what they have written to each other. (As always, one member of the group acts as recorder and later as speaker for the group.)

Journal entries provide a great place for students to explore possibilities for oral responses or for formal papers. To make the journals a safe place—free from concerns about grades—you might assure students that you will not be correcting or editing what they write in their journals. Instead, consider reading carefully what they have to say and responding with your own comments and questions. As you read students' journals, you might jot observations in the margins and then write a sentence or two at the end of each entry. Keeping these comments as affirming as possible helps students to develop confidence in trying out unusual or controversial ideas and approaches to writing. For instance, your comments might praise an intriguing insight, a perceptive observation, or a moving personal connection. Obviously, however, no instructor will admire or agree with everything students write in their journals. Sometimes, entries are boring, shallow, or even offensive. Yet suspending harsh judgment and instead asking questions or suggesting possibilities often leads a half-hearted or hostile student to engage in the class more positively and fully.

The journals provide a way to communicate with students each week in a private and safe setting. For instance, if you notice that a student seems uncomfortable during group work or during discussion, you might make a note in the journal, asking if you can be of help and suggesting that the student come to office hours or talk with you after class. Just as you can communicate with students through the journals, so, too, can they let you know about some aspect of the course that they are either troubled by or that they are finding particularly rewarding.

One way to handle journals is to collect them once a week and return them on the same day of the following week. To facilitate handling journals, ask students to write on loose-leaf paper and to submit just one week's entries in a pocket-type folder. When you return the journals, students remove the entries on which you have commented and store them in a three-ring punch notebook Then they place their new entries in the folders and hand them back to you. This process means that you carry home slim folders rather than heavy notebooks of varying sizes and shapes.

If collecting and writing responses to journals doesn't fit your course plans, consider the following possibilities:

- Do not collect journals, but instead ask students to bring them to class to use as a basis for discussion.

- Collect journals but return them with only a check mark to indicate "accepted" or a minus sign to indicate "needs improvement before I can accept it."

- Collect and grade journals, evaluating them in the same way an essay or research paper would be evaluated.

Journal work has many helpful side effects. For example, when students have to write on the assigned readings, they come to class prepared and having thought about what they've read. Usually, when you assign reading journals, quizzes are neither necessary nor useful. Also, because students are doing so much writing, they begin to feel more at ease with the process. Journals convince them that writing *is* a way of thinking, and many of them begin to be more comfortable with formal writing as well. Finally, journals provide a window into thoughts, hopes, and feelings that students might not readily express aloud in class. You have a chance to see what is really going on for them as they read the assigned selections, and these insights often can help to shape future class plans.

In addition to topics for journals that you generate or that your students come up with on their own, each reading selection in *Connections* is preceded by several prereading/journal-writing questions.

Collaborative Projects

Many of the extended writing topics that follow each selection work well as collaborative projects. Students might begin collaborations during small group meetings in class. During their first meeting as a group, encourage them to exchange names and telephone numbers to facilitate arranging further meetings.

When the projects are completed, each group might serve as a panel, with each member presenting part of the group's findings to the class. To accompany this presentation, you may ask for one written report from the entire group (a paper that would require a great deal of cooperation and coordination) or you may want each member of the group to submit a one- or two-page summary of the oral report offered during the panel discussion.

In-Class Essay Series

While organizing this project takes some time, it ultimately promotes a great deal of writing while keeping the instructor's correcting time to a minimum. During the term, students write a series of essays—perhaps three or four—taking about twenty or thirty minutes for each writing. These writings may be announced or unannounced. After each writing session, collect and alphabetize the essays; then store them in a large envelope or folder.

After all in-class essays in the series have been completed, collected, and stored (but not corrected), redistribute them to students during another class period. Then ask students to meet in small groups or in pairs to read one another's essays. With the help of peers, each student decides which of the three essays to rewrite and submit for a grade. If you ask them to submit the original essay along with the final copy, you'll have a chance to observe and comment on their revision process.

Topics that follow each reading selection provide possibilities for the in-class writing series.

ASSESSING STUDENTS' WRITING:
DEALING WITH THE SCARLET LETTER

The ways and means of assessing student writing are nearly as varied as individual instructors themselves. As a result, students are often understandably confused as to what good writing really is and may even note that one instructor will give a high grade for a piece, while another stamps a low grade on this same writing. Consider, then, the following objectives when you establish guidelines for evaluation:

1. Students should be aware of what you expect in any assignment. Class handouts or class discussion should focus on the requirements for all stages of writing (see examples A–E, this guide, pp. 16–20).

2. Established criteria should be appropriately balanced. For example, the content of a piece of writing should be at least as valuable as the mechanics of a piece (see example C, this guide, p. 18). (For most assignments, most instructors will see content and development as considerably more important than mechanics.)

3. Either verbal or written comments (or both) should complement the grade on a piece of writing. Such comments should aim to show students their strengths in writing as well as their specific weaknesses.

4. Students should be allowed to revise initial drafts.

Based on these objectives, consider the following assessment strategies related to two elements of the writing process—revision and final products. Students usually find direction and motivation through these options.

First Draft Assessment Options

*   *The Ungraded First Draft*
    In this case, first drafts do not receive a letter grade. Instead, the instructor either holds a one-on-one conference or writes marginal comments in order to direct students to areas that

deserve praise or require more reworking on the student's part. We also know an instructor who tapes comments while she's reading her students' drafts, and she's found much success with this method of feedback. (Students purchase a blank audio tape as part of their "books and supplies" requirement; they submit their writing in a pocket-type folder along with the tape; the few students who have no tape player can use one at the library/ media center.)

In order to avoid overwhelming the student (and, just as important, in order to avoid an overwhelming amount of time on your part), consider limiting comments and directions in order of importance:

High-order concerns: Content, Focus, Organization, Development

Middle-order concerns: Coherence, Style, Word Choice

Lower-order concerns: Usage, Mechanics, Grammar

- *Scaling the First Draft*
  As an alternative to the ungraded draft, we've found that many students like knowing where their writing falls within a certain range of writing expectations. In addition to writing comments on drafts, our fellow instructors have found success marking the drafts with one of the following possibilities:
  - check plus (✓+), check (✓), check minus (✓–)
  - Publishable, Revisable, Rewritable (see example D, this guide, p. 19)
  - An "If this were a finished product" grade (not figured into a student's final grade)
  - A 1/3 draft, 2/3 final-product grade ratio
  - A "process" grade that measures the apparent effort in composing the first draft

Whatever approach you choose to use, we strongly recommend that you do not correct the surface errors on student papers. By correcting such errors, the instructor ends up doing more work than the student. In addition, the student often fails to recognize his or her own pattern of errors. We've found the following options make students more responsible for their own editing issues:

- Put a check in the left-hand margin next to any sentence that contains an error in grammar or mechanics. In the beginning, we've found it helpful to give the student a hint at the error: P = punctuation; SP = spelling; a plain check means anything else.
- If a paper has one or two recurrent errors, point them out on half the paper, and ask the student to locate the rest.
- Correct one error and give a brief explanation as to what is causing the error ("This fragment is caused by an '-ing' word—it needs an auxiliary [helping] verb to make the thought complete"), and ask student to locate and correct any other errors of this type.
- Ask students to keep a record of the errors in their writing. Have them contract to rid their next paper of at least one of these errors.

Final Products

If you've commented on students' drafts (through either written comments, office conferences, or class workshops), reading and assessing final papers can usually be accomplished rather quickly. At this stage, you want to commend the student for any improvements in revising. You also want to give the student some helpful advice for future writing assignments.

In addition to short and clear comments, many instructors find an evaluation sheet especially useful in highlighting the strengths and weaknesses within a piece of writing. More importantly, students can immediately see the areas that deserve more attention the next time around (see examples A–E, this guide, pp. 16–20).

A Plug for Portfolios

In recent years, many instructors have switched from grading single papers to requiring students to submit a semester portfolio for a final grade. As in the area of assessment, there is no one way to use or grade portfolios in any classroom. However, one thing is certain: Many instructors who have switched to portfolio evaluation swear that this is one method they will use for a long time to come. The feedback from students has been positive, as well. We've discovered several methods that have worked well for both instructors and students.

Here are three sample options for a final portfolio's contents:

- Twenty typed pages, including (at the instructor's discretion, of course) formal essays as well as journal entries, creative pieces, reports requiring research, and so on
- Four major papers (three to five pages) written for the class, including the last formal writing assignment
- A minimum of thirty pages, including reading responses, art work, other class work, and choices from writing assignments

Final assessments on portfolios vary as well. Some instructors prefer to assign just one holistic grade to the entire portfolio. Still others assign different grades to specific criteria: amount of writing, growth in writing, final products, writing process, the selection process, the self-reflection process.

Whatever criteria you choose, keep in mind that collecting portfolios at a midterm point is a good idea, especially for first-semester freshmen. That way, students (and you!) aren't scrambling the last week of school trying to throw together a collection of their best writing. In addition, a sharing of portfolio entries three or four times over the course of the semester allows students to publish the pieces they most want to share.

Finally, many instructors have found that allowing students to take part in the assessment process (this applies at any stage of writing) makes them more apt to recognize their own responsibility for the final grade their writing earns. Consider questions like these to encourage students to think about what they have written:

- If you had more time, what would you do with this writing?
- What do you feel is the strongest part of this piece?
- What areas still might need more work at this point?
- What were some of the problems you encountered while working on this piece?

- What would you do differently the next time around?
- Assess your level of dedication to this writing: poor, so-so, average, zealous, etc.
- Assign this paper the grade you feel it merits.

Example A

BASIC WRITING—EVALUATION, PAPER #2: REPORTING

Student: _____   Title: _____

	weak		strong	
Focus:	( )	( )	( )	( )

1. Are the ideas in this paper clearly stated?
2. Is the thesis clear and narrow?
3. Does the writer cover one incident or event?

Development:	( )	( )	( )	( )

4. Does the writer explore the subject in depth?
5. Is there enough information contained in each paragraph?
6. Is there any unnecessary information?
7. Does each paragraph contain just one topic?

Organization:	( )	( )	( )	( )

8 Is the information in this paper organized in a logical, clear manner?
9. Is the introduction interesting and informative?
10. Does the paper conclude effectively?

Details:	( )	( )	( )	( )

11. Does the writer provide good, concrete details?
12. Does the writer use strong, active verbs?
13. Does the writer use clear, descriptive language throughout?

Mechanics:	( )	( )	( )	( )

14. Punctuation
    Fragments
    Spelling
    Agreement

Overall Grade/Comments:

Example B

THE WRITING PROCESS EVALUATION

ESSAY: _____   **Student Writer:** _____

Category	Maximum Points	Your Points
FOCUS: This essay has a clear idea or purpose; the introduction indicates the topic and direction of the essay; body paragraphs support the theses.	20	_____
ORGANIZATION: Ideas flow in a logical, clear manner; transitions are effective; conclusion relates to introduction/fulfills the reader's expectations.	20	_____
DEVELOPMENT: The subject is explored in depth; specific facts and details add vitality to the essay; all information is necessary.	30	_____
STYLE: The writer's manner is suited to the audience and purpose; words are precise; writing is strong and clear; sentences are constructed to enhance focus and add vitality to the essay.	15	_____
MECHANICS/EDITING: Sentences are properly constructed, punctuation is correct, subject/ verb and pronouns agree; the writer has proofread for spelling and typographical errors.	15	_____
OVERALL SCORE	100	_____

SUGGESTIONS FOR REVISION/FUTURE WRITING ASSIGNMENTS:

Example C

BASIC WRITING

ESSAY: _____   **Student Writer:** _____

Category	Maximum Points	Your Points
FOCUS: Paper deals with one topic or idea. Thesis is clear and controls subsequent paragraphs.	20	_____
ORGANIZATION: Ideas follow in a logical, clear order.	20	_____
DEVELOPMENT: Statements are supported through examples, vivid details, and facts.	20	_____
INTRO AND CONCLUSION: Opening paragraph captures the reader's interest and clues the reader as to the author's purpose in writing; conclusion sufficiently wraps up information; leaves reader with something to think about.	15	_____

GRAMMAR AND MECHANICS

	# of Errors	
Sentence Fragments	_____	
Sentence Run-Ons	_____	
Subject/Verb Agreement	_____	
Verb Tenses	_____	
Quotation Punctuation	_____	
Spelling Errors	_____	
	25	_____
Total:	100	_____

GENERAL COMMENTS, SUGGESTIONS FOR REVISION:

Example D

GRADING SYSTEM

Student: _____

WRITING IN PROGRESS/DATE: _____

PUBLISHABLE: The writing at this point has a clear and perceptive point. It is also well supported and developed with reasoning and details. The organization is effective and appropriate, as is the style of writing in this piece. Only minor spelling and mechanical errors still remain at this point.

   Suggestions:

REVISABLE: The idea behind this writing is good and shows considerable evidence of planning, but at this point, the writing needs more attention to one or more of the following areas: organization, adequate support and development, smooth transitions between major points, style, or mechanics.

   Suggestions:

REWRITE: The writing is unacceptable college writing at this point because of one of the following:

1. The writing makes no consistent or useful point. No clear purpose is evident.

2. The writing is poorly constructed and hastily written; the reader has trouble following the main idea.

3. The writing contains too many sentence-structure errors so that the message is troublesome to decipher.

4. The writing does not fulfill the assignment.

Suggestions:

Example E

SUGGESTIONS FOR REVISIONS

Student Writer: _____

Topic: _____

CLARITY: Thesis Statement/Introduction

INFORMATION: Development/Support/Organization

APPROPRIATE LANGUAGE: Tone, Correctness

PLANNING THE SYLLABUS

The structure of *Connections* allows great flexibility as you design your syllabus and as you plan for each class. Here are descriptions of the book's features and suggestions for ways you might use these features.

I. *Section One—Critical Reading and Thinking: An Approach to Crossing Cultures*

Whatever direction your course takes, this Section will serve as an introduction both to the concept of multiculturalism and to practical reading and thinking skills. See pages 1–6 of this guide for detailed teaching suggestions.

II. *Introductions to Sections Two, Three, and Four*

Each of these introductions provides an overview of the thematic readings included in the section.

In addition, each introduction focuses the student's attention on a particular aim for writing. Section Two explains writing to express ideas and feelings; Section Three addresses writing to explain; Section Four discusses writing to persuade.

Included are approaches for reading as well as examples of student writing that model possible processes for writing to express ideas and feelings, writing to explain, and writing to persuade. Because these sample processes introduce different discovery strategies as well as various approaches to drafting essays and to revising, you may want to assign all three introductions before you begin exploring various thematic readings. If students have read all three, they will have a fuller repertoire of strategies for reading and writing than they will if you teach each "motive for writing" section separately.

On the other hand, if you want to emphasize the aims of writing, consider assigning a Section introduction and then asking students to read and respond to reading selections within that section. This process provides students with an understanding of a particular motive for writing and, in addition, gives them examples of the possibilities writers have when they pursue that aim.

Whether you choose to teach the introductions to Sections Two, Three, and Four together or to assign them separately, each introduction should require no more than an hour of class time to discuss.

III. *Photographs and Previews*

Each thematic unit begins with a series of photographs that relate in some way to that unit's theme. Interspersed with the photographs are quotations from some of the selections in the thematic unit. You'll find specific suggestions for students to write about and discuss these photographs and previews later in this guide.

As a general teaching strategy, you may want to use these pictures and quotations as ways to encourage students to develop the prereading strategies of prediction and early response. They might write journal entries or brief warm-up commentaries in class suggesting what expectations, questions, issues, and concerns they'll have in mind as they read the selections you've assigned.

IV. *Prereading and Journal-Writing Suggestions*

These topics precede each reading selection and serve as a bridge from the students' own experiences and current knowledge to the ideas, feelings, and information the author offers. Like the photographs and previews, these topics provide opportunities for students to sharpen their predicting skills and, in addition, should serve to arouse interest in the reading that follows.

V. *Reading Selections*

Each of the nine thematic units provides a variety of selections that reflect a particular multicultural theme and, in addition, exemplify the motive for writing explained in the introduction of the section where that theme appears.

Nonfiction reading selections include essays, newspaper articles, transcripts of interviews, journals, reviews, letters, and excerpts from books. You may want to point out these different approaches to writing and ask students to experiment with various approaches in their journals (or in assigned papers, if you consider these approaches useful for the writing goals of your course).

In addition to nonfiction readings that relate both to the unit's theme and to the section's motive for writing, each thematic unit also offers a short story and a poem. Reading these examples of imaginative literature encourages students to think about the themes they are pursuing in different ways and, perhaps, to try some imaginative writing of their own.

VI. *Topics for Reading and Discussion*

Following each selection are topics you might use for discussion or for the basis of a writing assignment. Many of these topics encourage students to pursue the aim exemplified by the selection they have just read. If you prefer to have students work on one writing aim at a time, you might reserve those topics that suggest an aim different from that Section's focus for discussion or for informal writing, such as journal entries or in-class warm-ups.

VII. *Suggestions for Extended Thinking and Research*

These topics, which follow each selection, work well as group projects. Many suggest the option of oral reports, panel discussions, or debates to accompany—or even replace—written response.

Of course, many of these topics work equally well as individual assignments, and if you ask for research as part of the course work, you'll find plenty of possibilities here.

VIII. *Topics for Making Connections*

At the end of each thematic unit are writing and discussion topics that ask students to see relationships among the selections they've read. Like the Suggestions for Extended Thinking and Research that follow each selection, these topics offer many opportunities for group reports, panel discussions, and debates, as well as for individual writing projects.

To provide additional reading selections for these topics, consult the thematic cross-reference list at the beginning of each thematic section in this guide.

IX. *Rhetorical Index*

If, in addition, to stressing the aims of writing, you also want to acquaint students with the rhetorical modes, the text offers a rhetorical listing of selections on pages xxi–xxvi.

SECTION ONE
CRITICAL READING AND THINKING:
AN APPROACH TO CROSSING CULTURES (pp. 1–26)

The explanations, examples, readings, and exercises in this chapter provide the rhetoric of multiculturalism that will serve as a basis for reading, writing about, thinking about, and discussing the selections in the rest of the text. Depending on the abilities and interests of your students, you may want to spend from one week to three weeks working through the strategies and issues that this chapter addresses.

Students in some classes will easily identify themselves as multicultural; perhaps the class will include several international students or students from very different racial and ethnic groups within the United States. On the other hand, students in some classes may look around and evaluate their peers as all belonging to the same culture. Whatever the make-up of the class, you may want to encourage students to broaden their definition of culture (as suggested by "What Is Culture?" (text page 6). When students recognize that any given group of human beings is diverse in many ways and that they, themselves, are members of several culture groups, they often feel more open to studying and thinking about the concept of multiculturalism. (Exercise 1, text page 7 works well to explore this idea further.)

Because issues of diversity and multiculturalism have had great play in the media (and in the political forums of the 1990s), students may have strong opinions about looking at and paying heed to the astonishing variety of cultures within their college, their town or city, their state, and their country. To begin discussing these issues, ask students to write and talk about their responses to Horace Miner's "Body Ritual among the Nacirema" (text pages 1–5). Most students enjoy Miner's piece, and many, with a little urging, will create an "anthropological report" on an aspect of their own lives. The laughter that accompanies writing and reading the misconceptions and skewed interpretations that constitute these reports often leads to a willing suspension of the suspicion and wariness some students feel when

24

they hear the word "multicultural." Depending on the responses of the class to this initial discussion, you may want to further address questions related to their concerns. If so, consider assigning Diane Ravitch's "Multiculturalism: E Pluribus Plures" (text pages 471–483) as a basis for discussion.

  Connections tries to go beyond offering a collection of readings that reflect America's multicultural society. As the opening section suggests, most students have been exposed to the idea of multiculturalism, yet many regard this concept as just another remote philosophical vision visited on them by their teachers and textbooks. "Why Read and Think to Cross Cultures?" (text page 6) suggests many reasons for thinking critically in the context of different cultures. To encourage discussion of these reasons, ask students to use one or more of the topics in Exercise 2 (text page 7) as a warm-up writing or as a subject for a journal entry to be brought to class and shared.

RESPONDING

In addition to explaining reasons for reading, writing, and thinking across cultures, Section One offers strategies. To practice these strategies, students may first read "Reading to Respond" (text page 7) and then complete Exercise 3 (text page 12). Students might share their marginal responses and the resulting journal entries in small groups, noting similarities and differences in their observations. You may want to point out that they need not try to reach consensus. Multiple readers add new possibilities, and the group's strategy should be to open options, not to discover a single agreed-upon view. When they finish discussion and convene as a class, you might ask them to write for two or three minutes on their reaction to the group discussion. Were they surprised in any way by the observations they heard? Did they discover any new ways of looking at the selection? Did they change their original response in any way?

UNDERSTANDING

After thinking about and discussing their initial responses, readers need to delay the rush to judgment by returning to the text and discovering exactly what the writer is saying. This step is particularly important when the topic is controversial or when it is offered from a perspective that is unfamiliar to the reader; of course, both points are often true of writings with multicultural themes. To work on these skills, students may read "Reading to Understand" (text page 15) and do Exercise 4 (text page 18), which works well as a small group task. Exercise 5 (text page 19) may be done as a follow-up or as an alternative. You might ask students to summarize one specific essay, rather than give them the options provided by the assignment in the text. If all students summarize one essay, you could collect them, make transparencies for the overhead projector from some, and use them as the basis for a class on summary writing.

Understanding inference is extremely difficult for many students, yet failing to understand what is connoted or misinterpreting shades of meaning can lead to serious breakdown in communication and comprehension. To assess your students' facility with making inferences, ask them to read "Reading to Understand Inferences" (text page 19) and to do Exercise 6 (text page 20) as an in-class writing exercise to be discussed with the class.

EVALUATING

Most college courses and most professions require making evaluations, yet many students do not understand the difference between summarizing the author's ideas and making a judgment of their own. "Reading to Evaluate" (text page 21) takes them through this essential process step by step and Exercise 7 (text page 26) provides a way to practice the strategies they have just read about.

SECTION TWO
EXPRESSIVE WRITING

READINGS: ARRIVALS

Photographs and Previews (pp. 36–38)
Suggestions for Writing

Photographs

1. Besides the fact that they are taking an oath, what one generalization could you make that would appear to be true for every person in this picture?

    Choose three people in this photograph that appear to be experiencing slightly different emotions at this moment in their lives. What three emotions do you see from these individuals?

2. How might the situation and the feelings of the people in the picture compare/contrast to the picture above?

    Under what type of circumstances would such a scene take place?

3. Are the two people in this picture embarking on an experience in a new country or returning to a place they know well? How do you know?

    From their facial expressions and body postures, what do you think these two people are feeling at the moment this picture was taken?

Previews

1. After reading these four quotations, what reasons can you offer as to why so many people would immigrate to America?

2. If you were an immigrant traveling on your own to this country, what would your impression be? Do you see America as a place of drudgery, a place to "get rich," a place to fear, or a place of opportunity?

Cross-Reference List: Alternative Selections for "Arrivals"

Richard Frethorne, Letter from Virginia, 1623 (p. 39)
(Cross-Chapter Connections: "American Dreams and Creations")

This piece, written by one of America's earliest immigrants, provides a good starting point for this theme, both chronologically and thematically. Students, however, may find the language and syntax somewhat unfamiliar. Having students read this piece aloud or having them write certain sentences in today's language should alleviate any problems with comprehension. For example, a modern beginning to this piece might go like this:

> Dear Mom and Dad,
> I really miss you, and hope you both are feeling fine. I'm trying to feel fine, too, but, because of this lousy flu going around the campus these days, I've been feeling pretty weak and out of sorts.

Choosing this approach to interpretation also introduces students to paraphrasing.

In addition to introducing a very early arrival in the United States, this selection provides a thematic connection between many students and Frethorne himself, a connection most will have no trouble seeing. Like the author of this selection, students, too, have already experienced the end of one chapter in their lives and the beginning of another. The college experience is a prime example of an "immigrant" experience. Whether they live on campus or commute from home to school, they have left a familiar world and have come to one that is unfamiliar and perhaps strange. Thus, if they read first with the purpose of simply connecting with Frethorne's experience (the prereading questions prepare them for this), they may sense that they have a personal connection with what's to come this semester.

Although any of the questions following this selection work as whole-group discussions, Questions No. 1 and 3 work especially well when discussed in small groups. Students' reactions to Frethorne will usually be mixed. Was his emigration an unbearable experience, or was he caught up in self-pity? Remind students that as they express their differing views, they should support their reactions with examples from the text. For instance, rather than simply stating that the experience was tremendously harsh, students should provide specific details (only 3 out of 20 lived; only 32 now left to fight 3,000; Frethorne eats only peas and gruel, and so forth). Students who feel that Frethorne's tone borders on whining may note that he refers to himself as a "child," claims he has "nothing to comfort him," and has nothing to get in this new land but "sickness and death." You may want to ask, then, if his complaining is justified, considering the extreme circumstances.

Question No. 2 asks students to think about Frethorne's experience in terms of their own personalities. A written response works well here. Encourage students to aim for three or four reasons when addressing the "Why? Why not?" portion of this question. This process helps them learn how to support their thoughts as an important part of developing writing skills.

The last three questions for this selection ask students to move beyond the text and their own experiences—to use their present and prior knowledge in order to come up with possibilities. Why did people immigrate to Jamestown in the 1600s? What do students remember from their past history lessons? (Most early immigrants came as merchants, eager for America's "treasures." Many came to spread Christianity. Some came because—for one reason or another— they were outcasts in their own society.) Are Americans still adventurous people searching for dreams? Do many Americans still hold faith in God as paramount? Is the "outsider" still a significant figure? Raise these questions to help students connect America's past to present issues and values.

Certainly, the text shows specifically why Frethorne and his fellow immigrants had such a hard time. Sickness, the threat of hostile Indians, the scarcity of food, the different weather and land conditions—all were foreign to Frethorne. Many early immigrants came from cities and were unfamiliar with and inexperienced in farming. Combined with less-than-ideal soil and unpredictable weather, this lack of know-how assured that malnutrition would be one of their greatest hardships. To fully understand Frethorne's fear of "enemies," students will again have to go back to early history lessons. By the time Frethorne wrote this piece, Native Americans had recognized that newcomers would take over their lands. Instead of feeding students this information, however, you could ask them to consult one library source as they respond to Question No. 5.

Charles Ball, Slave Ship (p. 42)
Edited by Julius Lester
(Cross-Chapter Connections: "Rights and Responsibilities")

Many students are quite familiar with the Civil War and the issue of slavery in the United States. Most, however, have little knowledge about the journeys slaves underwent on the way to this country. This short selection provides students with a firsthand account of the atrocities that so many Africans endured at the hands of slave traders. Certainly the section describing young children thrown overboard should stir emotions. Ask students to discuss their reactions as well as their impressions of this piece, and encourage them to move beyond history with questions such as these:

- Could anything like this happen again today? In this country? In other countries? Why or why not?
- Why did the slave traders throw the children overboard? Are women, in general, more protective of their children than men are?

In contrast to the urgent, personal tone in the Frethorne piece (text p. 39), this short selection takes an almost distant, detached tone

(Question No. 1). To achieve this tone, the author uses passive voice in many parts ("Twenty persons were seized . . . and amongst these were three children"; "the other was taken up by some men"; "we were obliged to sit all the time"; "they were driven down amongst us"). Using passive voice reinforces the lack of power the slaves faced during this ordeal. You might ask students to change passive voice to active voice to demonstrate the differences such a change would make.

Question No. 3 also works well to help students consider tone. Why would the writer adopt such a passive tone? Here students may see that the specific incidents are enough to move an audience. In other words, they may recognize the power of the proverbial "show, don't tell!" advice so many of them have already heard from good writing teachers. In addition, students should recognize the connotation of power in words like "seized," "prison," "right," and "iron."

Question No. 2 asks students to use basic information to draw some conclusions. What do they know about the narrator? They know only that the speaker survived the trip and has been a slave for five years. From this information, then, what can they conclude? (He must have been strong and healthy, probably unmarried, for he never mentions leaving a spouse or children behind; he seems to have a strong sense of community since he uses "we" to refer to himself, and he also must have had a strong will to survive.)

The last two questions allow students to connect with the text in a unique way. They are asked to place themselves in this piece, first as a character and then as an astute observer with a good imagination. Most students find plenty of inspiration in these last two topics. Some will even discover something they may have thought impossible: Writing can be a pleasure! Students' writings on these selections will also provide useful and interesting examples to share. Consider asking students to read aloud (or to allow you to read aloud) passages of vivid description that demonstrate clear, engaging voices.

Pauline Newman, From Steerage to Sweat Shop (p. 45)
(Cross-Chapter Connections: "Ways of Learning," "American Dreams and Creations," "Rights and Responsibilities")

Because the prereading questions establish the notions of nostalgia and idealism, students, as they read, will readily identify with what

Newman left behind and what she dared to begin over a century ago. Before going back in time, however, allow students time to discuss modern social issues that might relate to Newman's view of the world. Raise questions to get students thinking about the state of Americans today: Do most really care about the country? About the world? Are Americans, in general, self-centered or other-centered?

After reading this selection, students will certainly recognize how "other-centered" Newman was. Perhaps the injustices in her homeland enabled her to see so clearly the injustices in the United States. Students will identify different specific characteristics in this author, but, in general, they might note the following about Newman: She was intelligent, honest (even blunt), confident, feisty, brave, loyal, moral, tough, and spirited. Ask students for specific examples from the text to support each claim.

To respond to Questions No. 2 and 3, students should refer to the text. For example, the third paragraph reveals immigrants' preconceived notions of America, with several examples indicating how Newman became educated. She "mingled with people," "didn't isolate herself," "listened," "read," and became culturally literate through attending plays and musical events. Students might make their own lists of those who have taught them about the various cultures to which they belong (friends, classmates, teachers, relatives, and so forth). In addition, they may consider books, magazines, or newspapers they've read on their own, as well as plays and concerts they've attended. Ask them to evaluate how "well-educated" they consider themselves in comparison to Newman.

Question No. 4 again asks students to search in the text for proof. This time, however, they are trying to discover whether the author supports her statements. Certainly Newman reveals that the poor during her time lacked the social programs that we have today. Welfare programs, disability plans, even a free, accessible, and universal public education were not available a century ago. The poor were subject to the rules of the rich. However, in the early part of the century many poor also had more hope in the future and more faith in the power of the individual.

Asking students to comment on the effectiveness of the ending urges them to become critical readers. Most students will recognize the power of the conclusion. However, asking them "why" the final sentences are so effective pushes them again to qualify their response.

Throughout this piece, Newman shows the courage early immigrants had as they fought for equality and justice. Future chapters in American history depend on her readers' actions and reactions, and she wastes no words in telling us so. Even though Newman's voice at the end suggests the maturity of an older person, the reader senses the fire and passion that still burn within her. After evaluating this moving conclusion, consider having the students reread—and reconsider—the prereading questions that ask whether or not they would be willing to fight for a cause today.

Students who do volunteer and work for a cause may want to cite specific details and examples from their experiences to refute Newman's claim that Americans today lack the passion and courage to work for change. (Of course, students will have to provide other examples as well, no matter what stance they take on this issue.)

Mary Gordon, More Than Just a Shrine: Paying Homage to the Ghosts of Ellis Island (p. 52)
(Cross-Chapter Connections: "Roots and Memories," "Crossing Borders")

Before discussing this essay, you may want to use the prereading questions to encourage students to talk about their own ethnic backgrounds.

Once "roots" have been established, students should recognize how many of their ancestors must have experienced the same feelings as Gordon's when they were processed through Ellis Island on their way to becoming "Americans." This essay offers an intriguing blend of personal narrative, imagination, and history—all resources that students have certainly been using themselves as they read and write for this course. Gordon uses rich, varied language, and if students underline in just one paragraph the words that affected them (words such as "deathlike" "swarming," "rejected," "adventurers," "suicides," par. 9), they'll see the choices available to writers and recognize the benefits of an extensive vocabulary.

After reading the text, ask students to consider Question No. 1 as a way of examining the options for introductions in their own writing. For example, Gordon certainly could have taken a historical approach to this essay. Instead, she opens on a personal note, describing an experience as a visitor in another country. Students may offer various reasons why she does this. The first-person approach indicates that she will probably focus on her feelings about Ellis Island instead of taking a strictly objective approach to the topic. The personal story also allows her to weave in her theme—the idea that Ellis Island is one of the few places where most Americans can feel a sense of unity. And the juxtaposition of different nationalities and the subsequent difficulties are, of course, why she begins with herself in a foreign country with another foreign visitor.

Based on the introduction, what can readers infer about this author? This part of the question allows students to see that as readers they engage in a relationship not only with a piece of writing, but with the writer as well. They may see that the author speaking to them is an astute observer (she notices the Russian licking his lips). She also is unafraid to make judgments (the Russian is compulsive) and, in addition, is quite proud of her family's background. Her heritage represents an important part of who she is.

Questions No. 2 and 4 continue examining the reader's relationship with the writer. How do students respond to Gordon's description of an American touring the country as a "Rotarian traveling in his Winnebago" (par. 4)? Is she making fun of the average tourist? Is her claim about commercialism justified? As students discuss their own experiences as tourists in America, they should be able to come to some (no doubt diverse) conclusions regarding the accuracy of Gordon's claims.

As students discuss the impressions most of us have of America's "founding fathers," they may see that many people accord special status to the first immigrants, although in actuality most of our ancestors came at a later time. As far as Gordon is concerned, Ellis Island solidifies the fact that this country belongs to her, not just "to the early settlers" and their descendants (par. 15). Students may have differing responses to Gordon's feeling that she is now a part of America's "national definition."

Gordon's final metaphor of the party is richly evocative. Ask students to extend this metaphor by posing specific questions related to a party, perhaps one they've attended since school began. Who is involved? What happened there? Why do people have a party to begin with? Through this general brainstorming, they may begin to see the richness of this metaphor:

- A party is a celebration, a place where different people come together, usually for the same reason. Ellis Island was the place where different people came together as well. And their coming to America was indeed a cause for celebration.

- At a party, people may feel awkward, unsure, and even scared. It's loud, noisy, a place initially full of strangers. Such was Ellis Island.

- A party is also an experience full of excitement, a place where a thousand conversations happen in all corners of the room. It's a room full of music and food, a room full of characters who are ready for a good time. Thus, the presence of so many different nationalities in our country adds spice and harmony to American life.

[**Note:** Some students may also see where the metaphor breaks down: for many, Ellis Island was not a party. It was a place filled with fear and anxiety, with poverty and disease, with those who were powerless at the mercy of those who held power.]

To encourage students to invent their own metaphors, ask them to complete the following phrases and then extend their answers:

- For me, living in America is like _____ .
- To me, America is a _____ .
- When I think of this country, the image of a _____ comes to mind.

Collect these responses and (with students' permission) duplicate several for the class to read and discuss.

Question No. 3 can serve as a quick warm-up exercise or as an extended essay, depending on your purposes. At the end of this unit, you may ask students to use one of these final questions as a starting point for personal narrative. Note, however, that the suggestions for Extended Thinking and Research at the end of this selection also offer the students choices for persuasive, objective, and creative writing.

Mary Antin, The Promised Land (p. 58)
(Cross-Chapter Connections: "Ways of Learning")

Unlike most of the pieces thus far in this section, this essay focuses on the wonderment and delight of the immigration experience. In many ways, this wondrous view complements the Houstons' piece, "Arrival at Manzanar" (text p. 63). Since both of these essays are easy to understand and reflect a positive outlook, you may consider having students read these two pieces together. Of course, in addition, "Arrival" sounds the ominous note of detainment and loss of freedom that contrasts strongly with Antin's sense of new-found choices and liberties.

The prereading suggestions ask students to slow down their writing and focus on details. To develop listening skills, you may ask students to write on No. 2 in class, and then in small groups read their pieces aloud. After listening to each selection, group members should ask each writer two questions related to the topic. This process also offers an excellent way to introduce revision before an extended essay is assigned. Discussion Question No. 3 also asks for quick thinking and use of details and would work well for small groups or as a pre-class, brief writing warm-up.

Antin makes clear her point that even though her new life was fraught with poverty, it was still preferable to living in Russia. Even rocking chairs and bananas can offer special pleasure, since they represent her new experience as an immigrant to the United States.

More than the material things she sees, however, the possibilities for choice and freedom are what matter to Antin and to her family. For instance, she views the opportunity for an American education as an astonishing, almost miraculous privilege. Some students may find this strange; others will agree with her view of school as a place of salvation and opportunity. You may want to ask whether—and why and for whom—education in this country should be a right or a privilege.

Like so many immigrants who arrived in the United States in the nineteenth and early twentieth centuries, the Antins are perfectly happy to change their names and to blend into this American society. As a matter of fact, they don't want to stand out as newcomers at all. If students were to emigrate to another country, how would they feel? Would they change their names and strive to assimilate in every way with their new culture? Why or why not? Expect plenty of controversy in response to these questions.

The last discussion question asks students to think about how the media portray the American family. Bringing examples of popular TV shows into the classroom provides an excellent way to connect discussion to present times and controversies. For example, consider taping a segment of a popular family show—"Roseanne," "The Simpsons," "Married with Children," "Fresh Prince," "A Different World," "Major Dad," "Home Improvement," and so forth. Have students take notes while they watch the episode and then in a whole-class discussion, compare the television family to Antin's family—and to real families today.

Jeanne Wakatsuki Houston and James D. Houston, Arrival at Manzanar (p. 63)
(Cross-Chapter Connections: "Parents and Children," "Rights and Responsibilities," "Crossing Borders")

The imprisonment of Japanese-Americans is a chapter in American history that has only recently become widely known. Most students will know facts and details about WWII, but few will have read about the trials fellow Americans endured because of their Japanese heritage. Houston writes in clear, engaging language, and the details she provides should both delight and sadden her readers. Although Houston says little about her father in this selection from her book, students should be able to draw the conclusion that he was a man who very much wanted to be treated like any other American. Imagine, then, what it was like for him to be imprisoned and labeled based on his Japanese heritage.

Questions No. 2, 4, and 5 ask the students to enter Jeanne Wakatsuki's childhood world. First, they are asked to be honest— would they become close friends with any or all of the Wakatsuki members? Of course, answers will vary and will perhaps be affected by students' cultural backgrounds. Whatever their response, most will acknowledge the young Jeanne Wakatsuki as a lively person with an irrepressible sense of humor and capacity for optimism.

Certainly, as a child, Wakatsuki was wide-eyed and honest. She was also a bit fearful and felt most secure at her mother's side. Despite her normal childhood fears, she looked forward to new experiences and she kept a delightful outlook in the face of tragic events. As she writes, when she went to bed that first night, she "had a great time jumping up and down on the mattress." A powerful and poignant detail that suggests her ability to find hope wherever she was.

And what was her mother like? Responses concerning the decision she makes to break her dishes will vary (Question No. 4). You may want to set up a scenario that puts the student in her position. What if a pawn broker, knowing you were desperate for money, offered to buy your grandmother's wedding ring for a pittance? How would you feel? If you needed the money, would you sell it? Why or why not? Understanding the mother's motivation is important here. What, if anything, did she accomplish by her actions? Let your students decide.

Question No. 5 also asks students to get inside a character's head, to connect in a firsthand way with the conflict at hand. Even if students choose only one scene to rewrite from another viewpoint, their older voice will serve as a significant contrast to the young author's voice.

After students read this child's-eye view of the internment camp, a visit to the *New York Times Index* for actual news reports on these camps might be a good idea. Students could work in groups on this project and report to classmates on the information they find. (You might ask some students to look for reports written during the years of World War II while others could investigate more recent reports.) Along with that, encourage students to read Houston's entire book, *Arrival at Manzanar*. The conflicts between Houston's parents when her father returns present readers with the horrible effects a family suffers when its members lose their sense of self, sense of pride, and sense of country.

Miguel Torres, Crossing the Border (p. 70)
(Cross-Chapter Connections: "Rights and Responsibilities," "Crossing Borders")

This selection and "A Boat Person's Story" (text p. 74) both provide short narratives explaining the struggles two people go through to leave their native countries and enter America. If you have students read these as a pair, they'll have plenty of opportunities to compare the theme, tone, language, and style.

Although "Crossing the Border" is quite easy to read, students should consider the inferences in this piece to get the full impact of

Miguel's experience. They will discover that what isn't said is often as important as what is overtly stated. Take the first paragraph, for example. To prompt students for Question No. 1, you may want to ask some questions that will help them set up inferences:

- What might it mean that Miguel lives with his mother and grandmother? (Absent father, perhaps?)
- What can you conclude about his working at the age of fifteen? (Formal education cut short.)
- What word do most of the sentences start with in this first paragraph? ("I.") What does this indicate? (Self-centeredness? Self-consciousness? Pride in self? Insecurity?)

Reading even one paragraph slowly and in detail helps students see just how much they can learn when they stop to ponder the implications of what they are reading. Now, most students will understand Miguel much better. He may have little contact with his father, his formal education is limited, and he may be self-conscious.

Students' evaluations of Miguel will vary. He seems to be a hard worker who wants to make his life better, yet he goes along with the plans of others and has few plans for improving his position beyond making money. He dismisses night school because he'd rather goof around after work.

Miguel goes from being scared to learning the ropes. He learns where to hide and how to act. He's beginning to understand the system and that makes him a bit more confident. Students may wonder whether Miguel might be better off just staying in Mexico City with his mother. Why doesn't he? Obviously, he earns little money there and besides, he's a young adult, ready for adventure. He's ready to leave home, to make his own mark on the world.

Nevertheless, few students will project economic success for Miguel ten years down the road. With little formal education and no desire to pursue education, Miguel shuts doors and closes off many options. He may be living in the United States, but chances are he will still be living close to poverty, near a big city.

Is Miguel's presence in America a hindrance or a contribution? Students will certainly be divided on this point, so you might see this as a grand opportunity to hold a debate.

- Divide the class into three groups—one group supports Miguel, one group wants him shipped out, and the third group is neutral.

- The first two groups have ten minutes to brainstorm together and write down their reasons. The third group should consult the text and write down all the facts it can in order to discern the truth.

- Allow each group five minutes to present its case and two minutes to rebut.

- When the groups have spoken, the neutral votes by a ballot to see where they—and Miguel—stand.

Vo Thi Tam, A Boat Person's Story (p. 74)
(Cross-Chapter Connections: "Men and Women," "Crossing Borders")

Students who read this piece in conjunction with "Crossing the Border" (text p. 70) will have little difficulty seeing the difference between these two emigration experiences. Although both narrators need to leave their native countries, Torres comes to America strictly for monetary reasons; Tam comes to save her life.

Tam and her family endure what few of us can even imagine. However, students are encouraged to think back to a time of tragedy in their own lives; they are also encouraged to think about our modern world and how much we have come to depend on modern technology. Whereas we just turn a faucet for water, Tam stood in line for hours, just to fill a rusty tin can.

Tam reveals so many hardships that students may have a hard time focusing on just one. The separation from her husband was painful; drinking sea water unimaginable agony. In addition, she suffered the horror of watching her mother and little boy on the verge of death and of delivering a baby in the camp.

How could people endure such experiences? Tam sums it up in her last line, really. She had been through hell, yet always focused on the hope of emigration. Certainly, at the bleakest points, many people gave up instead of fighting. Tam may have felt like that at times, too; however, she had four persons' lives on her shoulders, and she was sustained by the possibility that her husband was also on his way to the United States.

To understand what her life was like before the invasion, students will have to go back to the beginning of this piece. Since Tam's husband was an officer in the air force, they most likely had a comfortable life. She says they had "jewelry and radios and other things" from those days.

So why does Tam sound so matter-of-fact in this piece? Why isn't she ranting and raving about this experience? Consider, for example, the paragraph where Tam begins, "Everyone was sick and, at one point, my mother and my little boy, four years old, were in agony, about to die." Tam gives few details, and never, in this entire account, does she say how she felt. But does she even have to? Like the speaker in "Slave Ship" (text p. 42), she seems to be beyond tears, yet she does want people to know what happened. She wants people to know the harshness and horrors that many flee as they try to come to this country.

In relation to the Torres piece (text p. 70), you may want to ask students these questions:

- Why did the United States open its borders to some of the boat people from Vietnam but close its borders to many Mexicans?
- If you thought that Torres should not be permitted to work in this country, what are your feelings about Tam?

Through reading these selections, students will see that issues of immigration are complex and profoundly troubling.

Interviewer: Bill Moyers, Dreaming Big Dreams: An Interview with Bharati Mukherjee (p. 79)
(Cross-Chapter Connections: "Ways of Learning," "American Dreams and Creations")

The prereading questions for this piece set the stage for one of Mukherjee's main themes: the sense of belonging. Blending philosophy, knowledge, and experience, Mukherjee and Moyers discuss what enables a person to belong; they consider at what point a foreigner in the United States might feel that he or she is really at home.

While reading this piece, students should imagine that they, too, are in the room with Moyers and Mukherjee. They should wonder, when Moyers asks a question, how they might answer. This transcript allows readers to pause and ponder a question for as long as they like before moving on to listen to Mukherjee's responses. As students read her observations, they should consider whether they agree with her. Do they know what she means? Are her answers clear? What are her dreams?

Ambitious and searching, Mukherjee dreams of taking risks, of being her own person, of finding the meaning of her life and her place in this universe. And she dreams of always being able to dream. To what extent do students share this vision of letting go of their "old selves," of freeing themselves from old rules and obligations? Some, certainly, must have felt this way when they entered college for the first time: a strange new country where undefined—and perhaps infinite—possibilities awaited.

Mukherjee is quite passionate about letting go of her old culture in order to become who she was meant to be. Do those who hold on to their cultures remain static? Do they lose out? Students will be divided on their responses to Question No. 2.

Mukherjee eschews the view that a multicultural society—such as the United States or Canada—should be viewed as a mosaic in which pieces, although beautiful side by side, remain separate from one another. She prefers an atmosphere where people move away from identifying with a specific culture and instead, look at themselves and others as separate individuals who must find common ground that connects them rather than continuing to follow and support customs that separate them. To aid students in their search for an apt analogy, you can set up the following phrase starter:

> "Living in America with so many types of people is like living in/on/under/between/inside a . . ."

As they consider Question No. 4, some students may feel as if Mukherjee unfairly criticizes American pioneers. Others may believe she is simply being honest. Encourage students to give reasons for whichever position they take. In addition, ask them to think objectively about American pioneers: the Puritans, those who traveled westward, those who fought in the Alamo, those who explore outer space. And have them consider American artists as pioneers. Do any books, films, or paintings support or contradict Mukherjee's viewpoint?

Clearly, Mukherjee has disengaged herself from the roots that she believes bind her. She totally disagrees with the caste system in India, which separates people according to class. She also has shed any notion that as a woman she should be of lower standing than a man. However, she still believes in strong family ties, in the value of education, and in living a good and moral life. She holds on to the teachings of her culture that she has, after careful evaluation, come to admire and value while throwing out the rules that held her back.

As students seek to formulate their own views of Mukherjee, you may want to suggest that they summarize the main points she makes about America, Americans, and finding a place where one fits. In addition, have students look at the questions that Moyers asks of his guest. What type of person is he? What is his primary purpose in this interview? Does he achieve this purpose? Then let the students in on this same process. Have them write three questions they would like to ask Mukherjee—and then project her possible responses.

Abraham Cahan, I Discover America (p. 89)

From real-life immigrants, students now move to a fictional account of one character s arrival in America. In this short story, Cahan creates a magnificent character. He is a dreamer and a poet, a man who innocently believes his head is filled with wisdom. Before judging this character, however, students might stop to think about themselves. Do they, too, imagine things that are not so? Do they dream more than they act?

When readers first meet the main character, they see him engaged with the vastness and mystery of the sea. Why does Cahan begin this way? Students may speculate that the sea and its mystery suggest the surprises the new country holds for this traveler. The character, aware of the power of this force, stands in awe and in fear of this journey. So we see him as a poet yet also as a realist. He is not fooled by the calm waves: He has seen the sea at other times as well.

Not only does this character reflect on the sea, but he also reveals how important prayers and psalms are to his well-being. Clearly, he is an avid student of the Bible; he has memorized passages, and his memory serves him well in this time of fear and need. But then he flashes from his prayers to a woman named Matilda. What does this information tell us about this character? He is a devoted student, a prayerful man, and at the same time, thinks about practical concerns such as the bride who awaits him. Although he is consumed with book knowledge, he also anticipates the details of daily life experiences.

Perhaps he is on his way to America because the spirit of adventure has moved him. Perhaps he feels he has some calling to be here. Whatever the reason, while he is on his voyage, his poetic outlook keeps him from worrying too much about future difficulties. He turns to his psalms and verse when the sea gets too rough. However, such an outlook is of little help when he lands on shore. Now, with his feet firmly in place, he must see with his own eyes. No longer can he rely on words in a book to help him understand all that is so new to him.

Most students will see that the character has not been deceived solely by Gitelson and the tailor; he has been deceived as well by his own poetic notions. At the end of this piece, he discovers how alone he truly is and how vast this new land is to him. He recognizes that all of what he must learn cannot be found in a book. Instead, he must rely on his experiences in America to discover not only what this country is all about, but what he is all about, too.

Carved on the Walls: Poetry by Early Chinese Immigrants (p. 96)
(Cross-Chapter Connections: "Roots and Memories," "American Dreams and Creations")

These recently published poems are intriguing and mysterious for most students. If students have been keeping journals, ask them, in response to the prereading suggestion No. 2, to go back through their entries to find a sentence or a phrase that strikes them as particularly strong. Most will be surprised at the richness of ideas and words they have already collected. Ask students to volunteer to copy their sentences and pass them to you so that you can publish several examples for the next class period.

You may want to approach these poems mainly for the themes and images they hold. Discussing elements such as rhyme and meter may distract students from connecting with these immigrants' experiences.

What can we tell about these anonymous writers? In Poem No. 5, the writer reflects on the passing of time, mentions a "cool autumn,"

writes of "this long road." What type of a person is this? Students may
see the author as someone who is young, anxious, a bit scared, and
very much alone. The writer seems open and honest, a careful and
thoughtful observer.

The tone in No. 8 clearly differs from that in No. 5. Whereas No. 5
was almost quiet, No. 8 sounds hard and angry. No reference to nature
here. The poem is more like a stone building. Students may
sympathize; many will realize that where we live is often, indeed, a
matter of luck or chance.

Some immigrants may have omitted their names because they
feared reprisals from authorities. Others may have wanted to maintain
a private self while expressing deep emotion and distress.

In contrast to No. 5 and No. 8, poem No. 31 sounds almost like a
scream instead of a poem. The writer seems at her or his end. Patience
is gone. Time is too long and hope just a whisper. Students can
brainstorm for the possible ways in which these immigrants spent
their days. Certainly the hours must have passed slowly with little
means to alleviate fear, tension, and boredom.

Asking students to imagine the types of music that would fit
poems No. 35 and No. 38 is really an extended lesson in tone and
voice. You may ask students to bring in any tapes that seem to fit these
same moods. Based on the images in each one of these poems, the
music should differ. For example, No. 35 may have a loud, harsh
sound, while No. 38 would be much sadder and more mournful. Any
music played in a minor key would seem appropriate.

Even though each of these poems is unique, students should be
able to identify two key themes: that of imprisonment and that of
loneliness. All poems contain some holding place ("steamship,"
"prison," "America," "wooden building"), and all have images of
loneliness ("cold autumn," "prison," "streams of tears," "wailing of
cold, wild geese").

After reading these poems, students are encouraged to connect to
their poetic muse, to ponder their own experiences, or to investigate
an outside source that will give them more information about Angel
Island. Even if students do not actually do any of these extended
assignments, consider asking them to explain in their journals which
one they would do if they had to. When a formal essay is assigned,
such a reflection will perhaps help them to find a direction.

READINGS: PARENTS AND CHILDREN

Photographs and Previews (pp. 100-102)
Suggestions for Writing

Photographs

1. What might be the relationship among the three people in this picture?

    From the position of the child in this scene, what inferences can you draw as so how the woman feels about the child?

2. When you look at this photograph for the first time, what is it you first notice?

    What details in this scene are typically American? Which details represent this family's native country? After examining details from each culture, which culture do you feel is more dominant?

3. From this photo, what particular values do you think this family cherishes most?

    Imagine you are actually "inside" this moment. What are the sights, sounds, and smells you experience as an insider here?

Previews

1. After reading these quotations, which one piece would you now be most interested in reading? Why?

2. If you could draw one conclusion about parent/child relationships from these quotes, what would it be?

Cross-Reference List: Alternative Selections for "Parents and Children"

Tran Thi Nga, Letter to My Mother (p. 103)
(Cross-Chapter Connections: "Arrivals," "Roots and Memories")

Students know when they write letters to family or friends that they cannot include everything they would like. When we write letters, we are especially aware of our audience and the effect our words have on them. As students read this piece, they should keep in mind the emotions, the unvoiced thoughts that are racing through the writer's mind.

Is Nga sad? lonesome? angry? happy? As the first question indicates, the specially chosen images are often clues indicating how a writer is feeling. In the beginning of this letter, the tone is very cordial. Actually, Nga could be writing to any one of the friends she left behind. She is careful to explain things like what poison ivy is. She then goes on to explain why Americans eat ice cream. Writing about this everyday food and the color orange, however, brings her back to her homeland; as she explains, the color looks like "Buddha's robes."

Now the tone changes (par. 6). Memories have been stirred, and the writer's voice becomes lonesome and sad. She writes, "We are sorry for you and for ourselves" (par. 6). From this point, the mother is mentioned in every thought. The writer shifts from her "I" experiences to the "you" of her mother. Despite the sad tone, however, the writer displays a sense of hope. She ends on an optimistic note, "praying to be reunited" with her mother.

Nga describes simple things because she recognizes that her mother will be interested in the details of her daily life: plants, her home, her town, the foods. Through such description, Nga reaches out and invites her mother to feel a part of her family in America. Nga does not mention what work she does, nor does she mention any

American acquaintances. Her life, most likely, revolves around her family. Perhaps she desperately wants to hold on to her memories and her past.

It's difficult to tell whether or not Nga really believes she will see her mother in the future. Ask students for facts from the letter. The mother is old. She is also frail: Nga worries about how thin she might be by now. These facts suggest that Nga will not see her mother again. She may return to Vietnam, but that will be years into the future and her mother will probably no longer be alive.

Like "More Than Just a Shrine" (text p. 52), this piece contains a particularly powerful metaphor. You can aid students in extending the metaphor of the pond by asking leading questions:

- How big is a pond?
- How does it compare to, say, a lake or a river or even the sea?
- Where do we find ponds?
- How do you envision the atmosphere surrounding a pond?

With these questions in mind, students can begin to see the significance of the pond as an image of Nga's homeland. Ponds are small and still. The water is unmoving in comparison to that of a river. Ponds are also safe places, small enough to become familiar. Ponds can be found in many locales, but, in general, the surrounding area is quiet and peaceful, a place where people come to rest and think. A pond is quiet, unmoving, and its shape suggests a completed circle. These images reflect Nga's view of the homeland she may never see again.

If Vietnam is a pond to Nga, how might she see the United States? Have students brainstorm on this question. Some appropriate metaphors, along the lines of Nga's, might be that the U.S. is a tourist-infested Miami Beach, the wild Pacific Ocean, a Wave-tech pool, white water rapids, a hurricane. Clearly, Nga longs for her quiet, small homeland; "clear or stinky," it is still hers.

Harry Dolan, I Remember Papa (p. 106)
(Cross-Chapter Connections: "Roots and Memories," "Rights and
Responsibilities")

This selection, although easy to read, presents most students with
an uneasy view of the world. Life isn't always fair, people aren't always
good, and even the most courageous can fail in this country, especially
if they are black and poor. Idealism and realism come face to face in
this piece. As much as students may like to believe that anyone who
tries can make it in America, the scene where Dolan speaks to his
father in prison definitely challenges that view.

Before reading and discussing this piece, students may benefit from
sharing their responses to the second prereading topic. Consider
addressing the many different images the word *father* evokes by doing
the following class exercise:

- Ask students to write a one-sentence definition of the word
  father.

- Have students read their definitions. Most of them will be pretty
  much the same: "A male who produces an offspring,""a male
  parent," and so on.

- Next, ask students to do a free-association: When you say the
  words "good father," they are to write down the first three words
  or phrases that come into their minds.

- Then have students read their responses. Write the words or
  phrases on the board to suggest the diverse possibilities that
  come from each person's observations and experiences.

Now that students are connected with Dolan's topic, invite them to
get inside the author's head. The first discussion question asks for risk
taking, as the students are immediately called upon to make a
judgment. Urge them to look to the text, to find support for their
evaluation. Actually, Dolan refrains from generalizing about white
men. He does, however, think the white man at the party is "smug,"
and at a later point in the story, when he is young, he sees white men
as "important-looking" in their work hats. Other than these two
references, however, Dolan steers clear of making judgments about
white people.

Questions No. 2 and 3 suggest how important Dolan's mother was
to him. Yet if he has better memories of his mother, why doesn't he

write about her? Ask students to focus on the word *remember* from Dolan's title, and then have them suggest words or phrases they could substitute for this word. Someone will certainly say "knew." Careful consideration may suggest, however, that this verb is not really a synonym: Remembering is not necessarily knowing. Thus, this one word in the title implies that although Dolan remembers certain things about this father, he did not necessarily know him well. Perhaps he has memories of his mother and also feels he knew her intimately; he may not feel the need to explore on paper the details of their relationship. On the other hand, writing about memories of his father may provide a way for Dolan to "know"—not simply to "remember"—his father.

Although Dolan's mother dies when he is young, students get a deep sense of who she was. What details does Dolan provide us with? Ask students to search back through the text for specific words and phrases:

- "deep, continuous coughing"
- She only ate Delicious apples, she was small, "barely five foot."
- She whispered, she was thin, she called her son "Junior," and she always smiled at him. Even when she was dying, she made the effort to smile, and she puckered her lips to her son and daughter to indicate a kiss.

Ask students to write one sentence that summarizes what this woman was like: "She was a chronically ill woman who loved her children and who struggled to deal with what life had dealt her."

In the text, students will find details describing Dolan's father as well. He doesn't appear in this piece until the mother's funeral. Here, the father tries to be brave. The next image of his father is a flashback that shows him at work, splitting boulders. He worked hard; he was strong, proud of his work, and he smiled. Then we see Dolan's injured father. Now he is a man who is hurt, a man who cries, a man who fights, a man who becomes defeated. A one-sentence summary of the father, in contrast to the mother, might go something like this: "Mr. Dolan was a grateful man who wanted to provide for his family, but, unlike his wife, he refused to accept, and fought against, the blows he was dealt as he tried to make a life for himself and his family."

Students may offer conflicting views of the father's reaction on the bus. Freeing the woman was courageous and noble; slugging the driver could be seen as headstrong and foolish. Allow students time to express their feelings on this incident. Some may believe the father was justified in hitting the driver; others will condemn this response.

The last question leads students to Dolan's theme in this piece—a theme that extends beyond the stories of his youth. As a child, Dolan saw his father as both a hero and a loser. As an adult with some distance from his past, he now sees his father in a clearer light. He was neither a hero nor a loser. He was simply a man doing the best he could with the little he had. And the theme? Looking back at the white man in the beginning, Dolan leads readers to see his point: Sweeping generalizations fail to consider complexity and ambiguity and rarely lead us to the truth .

The first Extended Thinking and Research suggestion makes a fine connection to the first journal entry as well as to the in-class denotation/connotation exercise (on the word *father*). Students may find a certain sense of closure—yet also open new possibilities—if they write short essays or journal entries on any one of these topics.

Grace Ming-Yee Wai, Chinese Puzzle (p. 113)
(Cross-Chapter Connections: "Roots and Memories," "Rights and Responsibilities")

Like the Dolan piece (text p. 106), this essay focuses on the relationship between a father and a child. However—in contrast to Dolan's father—Wai's father was a teacher and a friend, as well as a strict parent, to his daughter. Since the basic topic deals with the father's role in his children's lives, this essay can easily be paired with "I Remember Papa."

Before having students explain Wai's relationship with her father, you might ask them to write for a few minutes on their own relationship with their fathers or other significant, older male friends/mentors. What do they do together? What do they talk about? How often do they spend time with one another? The purpose here is to set the stage, again, for answers that are neither black nor white.

For example, Question No. 1 asks about Wai's relationship with her father. Urge students to move beyond the quick response. "They were close" doesn't acknowledge the levels within this relationship. If students look to the text, they will discover the complexity of feelings between Wai and her father:

Par. 4:   Wai both fears and respects her father.

Family means everything to Wai's father.

Par. 5:   Father doesn't have much time alone with Wai because of his work.

Wai likes time alone with her father.

Par. 6:   Wai is afraid and wants her father.

Father makes Wai go to school alone, even though it hurts him too. He doesn't tell her this, though.

Par. 7:   Wai doesn't show her true feelings in front of her father.

Par. 9:   Again, Wai's father is stern with her about school.

Par. 15:   Wai is afraid of her father's reaction; father reacts with compassion and wisdom, yet never speaks his feelings.

Par. 17:   Wai is afraid when she sees her father cry.

She finds it hard to talk with her father.

Par. 19:   Wai hugs her father; he says for her to be good.

So what will students conclude about this relationship? Many will see the father as a good man who had little time with his daughter, and Wai as a good daughter who wanted more time with her father. They loved each other, but they seldom found the words to express it.

Responses to Question No. 4, comparing a Chinese family with an American family, will differ. Points to consider in this comparison may include importance of family, education, independence, hard work, and justice.

Questions No. 3 and 4 focus on Wai as a child. Students may reflect on their own times in school versus times with friends in the neighborhood as they consider No. 3: Sometimes children are more themselves in neighborhoods, whereas in school they might act a certain way to please the crowd. When Wai writes that she had a hard time seeing her father cry, she is beginning to understand that parents are not hardened statues who have all the answers. In some ways, their feelings are just like their children's: They feel sorrow, anger, and loneliness, too. It takes time and years for children to accept their parents' humanity and to recognize their vulnerabilities as well as their strengths.

The strong community presence at the funeral suggests that Wai's father was well respected and well liked by many people. He retained his cultural values while becoming an integral part of his American society.

Throughout this piece, Wai explores what her life would have been like had her father lived longer. If students go back to the first two paragraphs and paragraphs 27 and 28, they may find possible answers to Wai's question. Her father valued a good education, and Wai is well-educated. Her father valued hard work, and Wai has worked hard to reach her goals. As the later paragraphs reveal, Wai still incorporates much of her family's culture in her own life. Would he be proud of her and her feminist values? This is a difficult and complex question, yet a close look at Wai's first school experience suggests that above all her father valued giving his children a sense of independence. We may speculate, then, that he would have accepted—and looked with pride—both at the ways his daughter was like him and at the ways she had grown on her own.

Maxine Hong Kingston, Photographs of My Parents (p. 120)
(Cross-Chapter Connections: "Roots and Memories," "Men and Women")

Kingston's essay is full of luminous details. Students will enjoy this piece more if they read it at a leisurely pace, in a quiet, comfortable spot, for Kingston writes as if she, too, is being slow and careful. To help students grasp why these details are so important to Kingston and to good writing in general, ask them to do this exercise:

> To develop a "writer's eye," when you look at someone's face (someone important to you), imagine you are seeing that face for the last time. Then write about it.

That's what Kingston has done, especially with the face of her mother. She has tried to photograph it forever in words and to go beyond the replication—to see the meaning behind the details. Question No. 1 gets students thinking about audience. For whom was Kingston writing? Students may speculate that she was writing for her parents.

Some may say she was writing for Chinese-Americans or, conversely, for Americans who are unaware of Chinese culture. Kingston almost certainly kept all of these potential readers in mind. However, another audience she seems to be writing for is herself. She wants to capture the essence of her parents; she wants to understand where she, and her life, fit with the people who gave birth to her and raised her. As another possibility, you might point out that many accomplished writers do block out the vast masses and envision a few close friends when they are in the process of creating their art. Some writers say that if the writing pleases only this small audience (or even pleases only the writers themselves), they are satisfied. If you can, pull some quotations on audience from the book *Writers on Writing* (Jon Winokur, Philadelphia: Running Press, 1990) or *Shoptalk: Write with Writers* (Donald Murray, Portsmouth, N.H.: Heinemann, 1990) and share them with your students.

Question No. 3 moves to the symbolic value of Kingston's mother's diploma. Kingston starts here because so much of her mother's life is wrapped up in this one article. This diploma represents her mother's past, her mother's pain, and her mother's dreams. Certainly, the death of her two children and the ten-year absence of her husband are part of the past and the pain. The fact that she persevered, on her own and all alone, to become a doctor is part of the pain and part of her future dream.

Compared to Kingston's father, the mother appears a stoic, no-nonsense person. Paragraphs 3 and 4 give vivid details of her mother. Students may note that Kingston tends to focus on her mother's eyes. (If any students have tried the "look at this face as if you were seeing it for the last time" exercise, you might ask them if they, too, focused on the eyes. Why? Why not?) The mother's eyes, as Kingston notes, stare ahead; they are "spacy" and "do not smile." From these descriptions, what can students infer about the mother? Perhaps they see a wounded soul, yet a determined person who has a sense of what matters in her life.

Kingston's father, on the other hand, wraps his arms around his buddies, wears American hats, and "smiles in front of a wall of clean laundry." Only once, when he doesn't know his picture is being taken, does he not smile. From these details, we can infer that Kingston's father was a man who surrounded himself with friends, a man who saw this country as an opportunity. He knows that smiling conveys the conventional American happy mood for picture taking, yet he seems to be a private man who may hide his inner feelings under his hats.

From these descriptions, readers can infer that Kingston has deep feelings for both of her parents. She has great reverence and compassion for her mother; she seems grateful to her father and at ease with who he is. (You may want to mention to students that in other essays, Kingston shows more ambivalence toward both her parents than she does in this piece.) How the parents feel about each other is not so clear. The photographs are separate. Here, the students would need more information than Kingston provides in order to draw and support reasonable conclusions. The students will clearly see, though, how differently each parent coped with the changes in their lives.

The photographs also suggest cultural differences. In the mother's graduation picture, her gaze is direct and independent. She is not trying to look like someone she is not. She is not posing or putting on airs. She hasn't learned how to do that. In contrast, the father's pictures reveal a culture that depends on action, props, and poses. Are the father and his friend really happy? It doesn't matter to them or to their newly adopted American culture. The convivial expressions make for a good picture and capture an idealized moment.

Lewis P. Johnson, For My Indian Daughter (p. 125)
(Cross-Chapter Connections: "Ways of Learning," "Roots and Memories")

The first two prereading topics for this piece allow the students to reflect on personal experiences, and the journal is a good place to keep these thoughts. The third topic—one that calls for word association/listing—would work well if students shared their responses either in small groups or as a whole class. To draw conclusions based on dozens of words, students will need to group and categorize responses. Then they can formulate a thesis that answers the question, "What views do we (as a class) hold of American Indians?"

This piece works well when taught in conjunction with Maxine Hong Kingston's essay (text p. 120). While Kingston addresses how two cultures affected her parents, Johnson thinks about how he would like to see his daughter embrace her Native American culture. Who is Johnson's audience? Native Americans? Readers unfamiliar with Native American issues? Readers hostile to—or sympathetic with— Native American issues? In what sense might Johnson himself be part of the audience to whom he is writing?

To respond to Question No. 2, students should reread paragraphs 3 and 13. Although Johnson is careful not to come out and condemn the man on the beach, he uses the following words in connection with him: "fat," "white and soft as grub," "middle-aged," "moronic." Based on these words, students should easily be able to conclude that Johnson thinks little of this man. He is, in fact, making fun of him when he calls him "fat" and "moronic." Some students may see Johnson's reactions as appropriate. Others may believe that such terminology suggests that the author may be biased in some ways himself. (Would the man's comments be less offensive if he were slim, tanned, young, and muscular? Is the man's meanness evidence that he is "moronic"—or does that label make unfair connections between intelligence and bigotry?)

If students glance back to the lists they made for the third prereading exercise, they will have some basis for answering Question No. 3. For example, if students have already concluded that most of the words they associated with the word *Indian* have violent or derogatory connotations, then will probably agree with Johnson on this point. If they find that the prereading responses were fair-minded, suggesting complexity and a variety of views, then they may conclude that, as far as this class goes, Johnson is overgeneralizing.

Pushing students to ask "why" in a reading urges them to analyze both the writer's purpose and the implications of word choices. First of all, what does "theft" mean? What does it imply? Suggestions may include: something wrong, something harmful, something unfair. Are there details in this section to support each of these implications? Raise these same types of questions for the word *circle*—what is it, and what does it imply? Unity, closure, completeness—all of these terms are appropriate, and students may find examples in this section to support each term.

To assess Johnson's reactions to the powwow, again have students engage in close reading by targeting certain loaded words and phrases. Perhaps the most saturated words in paragraphs 9 and 10 are "masquerade" and "ridiculous." Students should be able to explore the connotations of these words using the process you've introduced.

Raymond Carver, My Father's Life (p. 129)
(Cross-Chapter Connections: "Roots and Memories," "Rights and Responsibilities")

Perhaps more than any other piece in this section, Carver's reflection on his parents is both compassionate and wistful. The first prereading topic asks students to write honestly about themselves, just as Carver writes honestly about his father. The central question that may best be answered at the end of the semester is this: "What does it take for a person to achieve his or her dreams in this country?" Carver's father was a victim of the Great Depression, yet many people survived this time period. What's the common denominator that provides us with happiness? Raising this question about the nature and possibility of the American Dream gets students thinking about one theme that ties together so many of the selections in this text.

From the opening paragraph alone, students should be able to infer that the relationship between Carver and his father was ambiguous. Their names indicate that they were the same, yet different. Carver likes the special name his father called him ("Frog") more than the name everyone else used ("Junior"). At an early age, he also feels quite free to speak back to his father, yet values the way his father listens to him.

Carver's mother remains in the background of this piece, and yet she is a stable force in her son's life. Why does she stay with her husband? Perhaps to answer this question, students need to see the question in a different light: "Why would any woman stay with a man who handled money carelessly, ran around with other women, and drank too much?" Carver's mother shows herself in many ways to be a strong person (par. 5, 11), and she was certainly not ignorant of her husband's weaknesses (par. 9, 13, 15, 16). In paragraph 20, however, we get a clue to her loyalty. In spite of all, she loves this man, feels sorry for him, or both. In addition, the photo she keeps (par. 29) reminds her who this man used to be—before the Depression, before he lost his "awkward grin." (Students who are familiar with recent psychological labels may observe that the Carver family is "dysfunctional" and that Mrs. Carver is "co-dependent." You may or may not want to pursue these rather facile categories. In all probability, you'll hear them in a class discussion sooner or later. If these terms do come up, you may want to ask students to define "dysfunctional" and "co-dependent" and to ask what insights they believe such designations provide. How do such generalizations work in terms of varied, individual lives?)

"Write about what you know," Carver's father advises him. What do students think about this advice? If students evaluate the successes they have had in writing, they may see that when they are deeply interested in a topic or when they know a great deal about their subject, they write more easily, clearly, and forcefully. Carver's father gave him useful advice. The younger Carver, however, did not see his father as capable of commenting on writing. After all, he didn't go to school; he wasn't trained in writing. Nevertheless, astute students may notice that the quality of writing in this essay suggests the wisdom of the father's advice.

As students evaluate their responses to Carver's father, they may benefit from taking time to develop their own definitions of "failure." They may also look back to their definitions of success (second prereading suggestion). According to these definitions, do they see Carver's father as a failure? Why would many people use this term to describe him? How can his failure be explained? Within this essay, many details suggest that external factors (the Depression, lack of education, living in poverty) coupled with internal factors (personal weaknesses with money and alcohol, psychological depression) were too much for Carver's father to overcome.

As he grew up, Carver spent more time with his mother, and he clearly felt closer to her than to his father. He talked with her more; he knew her better. The poem and the reflection on the photograph (par. 29) show how little Carver knew of his father and how much he longed to understand more. The fish and the beer (Question No. 6) are central images, at least to Carver, of who his father was. Together, these images reflect a carefree, happy-go-lucky young man, a simple man. The fish may also symbolize early success and confidence while the beer, in contrast, foreshadows his greatest nemesis. (Here, students might compare the photographic images Carver describes with the images Kingston discusses in "Photographs of My Parents" [text p. 120]).

Ask students to locate the tender images in Carver's poem ("sheepish grin," "he would like to pose brave and hearty," "old hat cocked over his ear"). In contrast, looking at the images that connote failure and loss of hope, however ("limply," "dead perch," "bottle of beer"), suggests the reasons Carver can't thank his father. He cannot be thankful for the things he sees as representing his father's destruction.

The Extended Thinking and Research suggestions give students an opportunity to deal with their own questions and complexities. Many students know the effects of alcoholism first hand. An objective research paper on this topic may help to address any unanswered questions they have. In addition, many students struggle with their relationship with a parent. The fourth topic might work well as a group debate. Students will have to determine their image of a good father—they may want to go back to Dolan's essay (text p. 113) and Wai's essay (text p. 106) to confirm or revise earlier definitions—and then hold group discussions based on the details and examples Carver provides in this piece.

Bharati Mukherjee, Fathering (p. 137)
(Cross-Chapter Connections: "Men and Women," "Rights and Responsibilities")

All three of the prereading questions directly connect with the major themes in Mukherjee's short story. Encourage students to discuss what they know of the Vietnam experience. Older students can be especially helpful in such discussions as many of them have views that come both from living through the Vietnam era and from hearing the "visions and revisions" that the media, as well as historians, veterans' groups, and numerous politicians, have offered since the war ended. You might begin by asking students to make a list of the images they have of the Vietnam War as well as a list of questions they have regarding this time period. Question No. 3—"Am I My Brother's Keeper?"—provides a useful prompt for journal writing or for a five- to ten-minute warm-up writing prior to discussion.

In addition to sharing prereading responses (or even better, before students do these activities), consider showing in class just one scene from a movie or documentary about the Vietnam War (see the first Extended Thinking and Research suggestion for examples). By viewing one graphic scene, students will already be caught up in the experience of Jason and his daughter, Eng.

The first discussion question should evoke widely varying responses. Some students may be turned off by the informal language; others may be offended by the relationship between Jason and Sharon; still others may be repelled by Eng's character. On the other hand, many students may find this story honest, refreshing, and bold. A whole-group discussion on this question helps students to see that readers' responses are almost never uniform. The details that impress and astonish one reader may offend another, while a third will simply express boredom and lack of connection with the themes and characters that have moved others to strong reactions.

Like the first discussion question, the second and third ask students to think of the three main characters in a subjective way. What characters do they like? Dislike? Why? Some readers may see Jason as an egocentric male in the middle of a mid-life crisis; some may see Sharon as a selfish, unsympathetic woman; others may see Eng as a manipulative child. The more students feel free to take risks as they speak, the more engaging the class discussion will be. Being able to give advice to these characters is one way of handing power over to the readers. "Sharon should dump the guy" or "Sharon should try to love Eng" are responses that connect the students to the possibilities within a fictional piece.

To answer whether or not Jason can succeed with Eng, students should carefully evaluate the facts in the story. First of all, what kind of a father has Jason been in the past? What are his strengths? His weaknesses? What problems does Eng have? Is Jason qualified to help her? And what about Sharon? Does Eng need a mother as well as a father? All of these questions should aid the students as they attempt to form a plausible answer to this problem. The last sentence will suggest to many that Jason will not be able to succeed—in the end, he is still living in a dream state, running away from himself and his problems.

The Extended Thinking and Research suggestions for this piece link up well with the prereading topics. If students found they knew little about Vietnam and want to know more, Suggestions No. 1 and 3 allow them the opportunity to further explore the Vietnam era. If students wrote passionately on the father's role in previous entries or if they found themselves upholding the "brother's keeper" philosophy, then Suggestion No. 2 fits well with their prereading thinking.

Cathy Song, The Youngest Daughter (p. 144)
(Cross-Chapter Connections: "Rights and Responsibilities")

Song's poem offers a different view on the parent-child relationship and addresses an issue with which more and more children are going to be faced: taking responsibility for aging parents.

Initially, students may find this poem difficult. You can help them understand that really exploring a poem means going back to it time and time again. The first encounter with a poem may be like meeting a new person. We have a first impression, but we don't know this individual well yet. One way to demonstrate this process is to have students write about their initial reactions immediately after reading the poem to themselves. Then you read the poem aloud. Next ask students to write again. What new insights do they now have? Did they notice details they had overlooked before? Did they understand a line differently? Once students have shared these first impressions, they are ready to work with the specifics.

Hard and painful images could include the following: "dark," "drying sun," "parched," "burn," "aspirin," "migraine," "pain," "flares," "graveled," "gruff," "sour taste," "old man," "bruises," "injecting insulin," "sunless." If students group these images, they may see three categories emerge—sickness, darkness, and oppressive heat. Based on these images alone, they should be able to sense the speaker's view of this time in her life and in her mother's life.

Focusing on the opening lines leads students to consider the theme and the tone of this piece. "Darkness" may symbolize evil, the lack of hope, the lack of wisdom, the absence of freedom, or the fear of the unknown. "For many years" lets the reader know that this situation has existed for a long, long time.

Song graphically describes her mother, from her voice to each freckle on her body. The image of her "great breasts/floating in the milky water/like two walruses . . . whiskered around the nipples" may amuse some students; it may disgust others. Some may read these lines as tender and poignant; others may see them as disrespectful. Children are not used to viewing their parents' bodies nor are they used to bathing their parents. The strangeness of this situation evokes varied responses; clearly no one of the readings suggested above is "the truth," yet neither can any of them be dismissed as farfetched or impossible.

In her own way, the elderly mother does still try to do things for her daughter. She rubs her head when she has a headache, and she makes afternoon tea. The daughter seems grateful for the massage, but the tea ritual is disturbing. Perhaps is it too strong a reminder of old routines, or maybe its silence suggests the infinitely long silence of death.

The image of "silence" here deserves some attention. Except for the mother's breathing and talking and splashing, there is little noise in this poem. The speaker is extremely quiet. The "silence" is all she can muster at this point. She goes through the motions, yet has lost the verbal part of communicating with her mother. Some readers have also observed that until the mother enters her final silence, the daughter cannot join the conversation of normal life.

Many students will find this poem disturbing. The images are bleak and the breeze outdoors provides the only hint of release. Taking care of an aging parent is a difficult situation for the child and the parent alike. To understand just how different cultures view the process of aging and the relationships of adult children with aging parents, groups of students could pick a specific culture and report back to the class with their findings. The third Extended Thinking and Research suggestion may lead to an argumentative essay or it would work well as a topic for an in-class debate.

READINGS: WAYS OF LEARNING

Photographs and Previews (pp. 148–150)
Suggestions for Writing

Photographs

1. From this photo, which character do you think is talking, and which one do you think is listening?

Assume that this photograph depicts the essence of learning. What factors, then, are critical to the learning process?

2. Is this activity taking place in a school yard or possibly somewhere else? Explain your answer.

From the facial expressions of the students, how do you think they feel about this activity?

3. What does the act of painting seem to mean to the woman in this photograph?
What are three possible reasons why this woman appears so pleased in this picture?

Previews

1. What conclusions can you draw from these quotations as to what the best conditions might be in order for true learning to take place?

2. What conditions or circumstances might interfere with a person's will to learn?

Cross-Reference List: Alternative Selections for "Ways of Learning"

Selection	Text Page
The Promised Land	58
Dreaming Big Dreams: An Interview with Bharati Mukherjee	79
The Site of Memory	223
Shanghai Blues	293
Bilingual Education: The Key to Basic Skills	499
Bilingual Education: Outdated and Unrealistic	503
What's Wrong with Black English?	532
What Means Switch (fiction)	536

Frederick Douglass, Learning to Read and Write (p. 151)
(Cross-Chapter Connections: "Rights and Responsibilities," "Crossing Borders")

In this essay, Douglass explains how he was able to learn without the help of a teacher. Most students are far more familiar with the traditional way of learning in a classroom, and thus Douglass's experience should raise the question: How exactly does one learn? Certainly processes differ among individuals, and students should try to be especially aware of their own learning patterns. You can help students understand how complicated learning can be by asking them to do the following exercise:

Exercise: Examining The Learning Process

- Think about something you can do well. (Nearly everyone can do at least one thing well, perhaps in the field of music, sports, the arts—or maybe a skill learned at work or in a volunteer activity.) Some students may see themselves as expert peacemakers, planners, arguers, listeners, or bargainers. Others may excel at shopping, playing a particular video game, or reading mystery or romance novels.

- Imagine that, as the expert in your field, you must teach this skill to the class. What would be the very first ten-minute lesson you would teach? To be a success in this venture, what must your students do or think about first?

- As the expert, write out your mini-lessons. (This can also be done in groups, with students deciding which skill the group would like to teach.) Be creative in your methods—will your lesson include hands-on work? Audio-visual presentations? A guest expert? Lecture? Discussion? Writing? Reading? Assessment—either by the teacher or by the learner?

- Volunteers may present their mini-lessons, or have each group present its mini-lesson to the class. All students will submit their lesson plans in written form—perhaps as reports, perhaps as journal entries.

After students get in touch with the ways people can learn, they are ready to evaluate, discuss, and write about the power of education. Douglass writes, "education and slavery were incompatible with each other." Thus, in answer to Question No. 1, Master Hugh's wife realizes when her young black slave reads the paper that the world and all its ideas are open to him. Once people can understand the written word, they can no longer be excluded from a very wide base of information.

Ask students if they can remember when they learned to read and how they felt. Many will remember feeling a part of a larger and older group. Some may also remember that once they could read, parents could no longer spell out words to keep secrets.

Douglass knew that in order to continue his learning, he needed teachers of some kind, so he sought out white boys. Why did he do this? Almost certainly the other black boys couldn't read or write either, so the white boys of the streets were his best hope. They may have been a different color, but they were young and poor like Douglass, and, in return for their lessons, Douglass could give them food from the house. They were hungry for food; he was hungry to learn.

Perhaps the most important thing Douglass gained through the books he read was that he had the ability to learn and with this ability came his first step toward freedom—both physical and intellectual. As he read the "Columbian Orator," Douglass realized that the slave could be just as smart as the master. Through Sheridan's speeches, Douglass came to understand that slavery was wrong and also to articulate clearly reasons why slavery was immoral. In the end, Douglass realized that since he now knew the truth, he was bound to uphold it; that is, he could no longer tolerate slavery and the chains, literal and figurative, that it imposed.

Question No. 4 invites students to discuss the responsibilities (perhaps perceived as burdens) that knowing the truth often imposes on each one of us. Students may be willing to share personal experiences as a preface to considering the "truths" of our times and their responses to those "truths." For example, how does knowing about the number of nuclear weapons in the world make them feel? How does knowing about environmental problems or the spread of AIDS make them feel? Do they, like Douglass, feel bound to action in any of these cases now that they know what they believe to be the "truth"?

Most students will identify with Douglass's metaphor of "light . . . by degrees." For the most part, we all learn step by step. Rarely is a certain concept or skill learned all at once. Encourage students to experiment with their own images for learning by asking them to complete the following sentence:

For me, learning to _____ (difficult skill or subject they have now mastered) was like _____.

Douglass's writing instruction was, of course, much different from ours today. His first piece of paper is a piece of timber in the shipyard, and he learns by watching and imitating. He also learns to write by turning the process into a game, a competition with another boy who could write well. In addition, students may note that while some individuals today strive to find clever ways to avoid learning, Douglass was forced to trick his "teachers" into yielding the information they held.

The last question expands on the exercise for thinking about the learning process at the beginning of this discussion of Douglass's piece (this guide, p. 63). Thinking through steps asks students to write a process essay. However, just listing steps and then peer conferencing with one another is another way to encourage students to recognize any essential details they may have excluded from a process.

The Extended Thinking and Research suggestions move students away from their own experiences and ask them to learn more about the history that has affected the country in which they live. Since this section of the text moves students from personal to explanatory writing, consider having them compile a bibliography that includes sources they could consult if they were researching and responding to one of the Extended Thinking topics.

Alfred Kazin, Brownsville Schooldays (p. 157)
(Cross-Chapter Connections: "Arriving," "Rights and Responsibilities")

This essay should be popular with most students, for it takes readers back to think about their own earlier experiences with education. The prereading questions set students up to think honestly about their hopes and expectations versus the reality of their educations. They are also asked to think about the type of student they believe they were and are. Such questioning connects the students not only to Kazin's experience, but to their past and present learning experiences as well.

The first question pushes students back to their earliest school days, asking them to revisit the places, people, words, actions, and reactions that composed their first school experience. Kazin says his school gave him the "shivers"; encourage students to think of one powerful, precise word that describes their first school experience. If they can do this, then they have focused the theme for their response to Question No. 1. For example, if the word chosen is "huge," then the experiences and people in this essay should all revolve around how big everything seemed—the school this writer evokes would be filled with physical, intellectual, and emotional barriers and challenges.

Kazin's word "shivers" suggests his theme. Most students will recognize, first of all, that he was scared. His first experience is filled with fear. "Shivers" also implies coldness; certainly fear and coldness lie at the heart of this essay. Kazin describes his teachers as the epitome of coldness and callousness. In response to Question No. 2, students may note that the teachers expected all students to be proficient and obedient—and not necessarily in that order. They also expected students to care about how well they did in relation to others in the class and to strive always for the highest grade. Students' responses to whether or not these expectations are unreasonable will vary. Most views will fall somewhere in the middle. To explore whether these expectations are useful later on in life, you might ask students what they believe a grade on a test or a paper teaches them. Have them think about whether education is about striving for an accumulation of grades or an accumulation of knowledge. How do they see the relationship between the two?

Comparing definitions of a "good" student might be interesting at this point in the semester. Does "good" mean anything besides "obedient" and "proficient"? Can you be a "good" student and skip classes? Can you be a "good" student and fail an exam?

Exploring these questions should suggest to students that defining a sound education is harder than it appears. What should a good educational atmosphere be like? When Kazin says that his atmosphere of learning was "fake," he means that who he was expected to be and what he was expected to master were disconnected from what he saw as the real world and from what he believed were valuable ideas. Grades, he would probably say, border on "fake" because they are ultimately subjective in many cases. The teacher/student relationship might be viewed as "fake" when it is based on power instead of mutual respect.

To explore the implications of a "fake" education, ask students in what ways the very building and classrooms themselves might be "fake," either as described in this essay or as they have experienced them. How are teachers "fake," and how are students "fake"?

Are there absolute answers to most questions? To some questions? To any questions? The "little white-haired Irishman" who taught civics would say that his answer was the only right answer. He also believed in competition between classmates. For him, learning was a battle, a war between right and wrong, one side against the other. Many students will know that educators today still debate the question: Does competition or cooperation foster learning best? If students recall and discuss their best learning experiences, they will see how complex this issue is and will understand why experts still disagree on the "right" approach.

The last question raises an intriguing paradox. In this piece, Kazin implies that his school days hindered his learning. However, he ends up being a successful writer. Clearly the Brownsville experience was a hindrance while he was there. His mind was kept closed, in a way, and all of his sights were on making the grade. But were there several advantages to Kazin's experience? After all, he did learn facts, and he did learn how to memorize those facts (whether or not that might contribute to the development of a strong writer is up for discussion). Most of all, however, he took this frightful experience and he survived despite it all. He learned to play the game, he learned to seek the truth, and he learned what he believed real education was all about.

Judith Oritz Cofer, *Casa*: A Partial Remembrance of a Puerto Rican Childhood (p. 166)
(Cross-Chapter Connections: "Roots and Memories," "Men and Women")

In contrast to Kazin's piece on the influences within the public education system, Cofer focuses on the learning that occurred through her relationships and experiences at home. Instead of recalling school experiences, then, students now shift to what their home lives might have taught them.

In general, Cofer's life was extremely family oriented. Rocking chairs passed from one generation to another as did stories that created the definition of "a Puerto Rican woman." If there is one moral to the stories Cofer remembers, it is that women should proceed with caution as far as men are concerned and that they must be strong, for men can be slyer and more powerful than women.

The story about Maria Loca is, of course, the tale of a young girl blinded by love and duped in the process. She was taken in by a young man's promises, forgetting to remember how manipulative a man can be when he is really feeling the pangs of lust, not love. Is the moral still applicable today? If students have developed a closeness and trust at this point in the semester, expect a heated exchange on this point.

Are the women merely "male-bashing" in this piece? As Cofer writes, the kitchen area "belonged only to us women," so some students may see these women's stories as parallel to men's "locker room" talk. For another view, however, ask students to think about the purpose the women had in mind as they passed down and embellished the stories. Certainly, entertainment was one factor. Teaching the young women what the older women had learned was the greater purpose, however. Some students will suggest that the women didn't congregate to put down men; they congregated to support one another.

Of course, the story of Maria that threads throughout this piece keeps readers, as well as the young Puerto Rican women, waiting for the lilting, touching ending. Although some students may see Mama as making fun of Maria, she isn't; the story is really a parable. Mama just breaks the tension, allowing laughter to be the healing agent in the room. Life is serious, the Puerto Rican women have discovered, yet, in this kitchen, they have found plenty of room for shared laughter.

Maya Angelou, Finishing School (p. 171)
(Cross-Connections: "Rights and Responsibilities," "A Question of Language")

Earlier selections in this thematic section show learning taking place in the streets, in the classroom, in the home, and now, in Angelou's remembrance, we see learning in the workplace. The subject matter in this piece differs as well. If students have read any of the previous pieces, ask them what the narrator was striving to learn. In Douglass's case, he yearned to read and write. Kazin yearned to think on his own. Cofer learned about relationships within her culture. And Angelou? Among other, sometimes harsher, lessons, she learned to respect herself. (As students begin reading, you may want to remind them that Maya Angelou is the name taken by the woman who began life as Marguerite—or Margaret—Johnson.)

At the beginning of this piece Margaret works in a white woman's home. To prepare for what both whites and many blacks in her community would have viewed as her main opportunity for future employment, she sets out to learn chores such as setting the table and preparing a full-course meal.

Angelou gives a precise and engaging description of her employer, Mrs. Cullinan. Students should have no difficulty picking out the details that describe this woman. Paragraph 3 describes her physical characteristics, paragraphs 4 and 5 describe her personality and demeanor, paragraph 9 describes some of her habits, and paragraphs 33–38 reveal the beliefs and emotions that form Mrs. Cullinan's mind and spirit.

She is a woman who has inherited her ancestors' traditions of Southern manners and, more importantly, she accepts without question their views of the differences between whites and blacks. In many ways, Mrs. Cullinan plays out her role as if she were the white slave owner of her grandparents' day (par. 6). Glory, in many ways, fills the part of the grateful slave. Thus, Glory's glass, as well as Margaret's, sits on a shelf separated from those used by the white family and their guests.

Although Mrs. Cullinan is spotlighted in this piece, Margaret's personality comes to light as well. Initially, she feels sorry for Mrs. Cullinan. At this point, Margaret is still a "beginning student" in this school. She is intrigued by Mrs. Cullinan and tries to imagine how painful it must be for her to go through life ugly and without any children. As she describes Mrs. Cullinan and her house, Margaret uses an intriguing fantasy motif, calling her place of employment an "Alice in Wonderland house." The topsy-turvy world further reveals itself when her employer refuses to call Margaret by her own name. Like the Queen of Hearts, Mrs. Cullinan insists on calling those whom she sees as inferior by any name she pleases (Question No. 7).

Glory, the third woman in this "school," has also had her name changed by Mrs. Cullinan, but, unlike Margaret, Glory accepts the change. In this acceptance, she has also acquiesced, at least on an external level, to Mrs. Cullinan's insistence on separation and levels of authority and power (Question No. 7). While social change may account in part for Glory's and Margaret's different responses, the greater reason for the difference in attitude between the two black women seems to be their backgrounds. As Angelou says, Glory was "a descendant of slaves" who had worked in this household for a long time. On the other hand, although Angelou almost certainly had ancestors who had been slaves, she lived with a grandmother (whom she and her brother called "Mamma"). Angelou's family had a strong sense of independence, rather than a tradition of uncomplaining service. Margaret knew her grandmother would let her quit this situation if she had good reason.

The Alice in Wonderland reference in this piece works on several levels. The world into which Alice falls when she stumbles into the rabbit hole makes no sense. Those who hold power hold it for no reason, and they abuse their power in astonishing ways. Mrs. Cullinan is cast the role of the ugly, mean-tempered Queen of Hearts who controls everything and everyone around her; Margaret then becomes Alice, the one who questions, does her best, and eventually, rebels, revealing the absurdity and unfairness of the Queen's court. Of course, further play with this analogy connects Glory to the nervous White Hare, Bailey becomes the caterpillar who offers Alice advice, and the dish-breaking ceremony parallels the Mad Hatter's tea party!

Mike Rose, I Just Wanna Be Average (p. 176)
(Cross-Chapter Connections: "Rights and Responsibilities," "Crossing Borders")

Like Alfred Kazin (text p. 157), Mike Rose writes about his experiences in public school and describes in detail the terrifying muddle of public school policies. A comparison of the teachers and techniques in this piece, in Kazin's essay (text p. 157), and in Gage's account (text p. 188) should lead to intriguing insights and varied opinions.

As the prereading questions indicate, this piece prompts readers to think about the issue of academic labeling and how this nearly universal practice affects the student's self-concept and motivation for learning. As Rose's title suggests (Discussion Question No. 1), students who are labeled as "losers" in school often remain satisfied with just getting by, just being average. Student who are told early on that they have little potential and few talents rarely aspire to be better. Instead, they remain on the track where they began or—perhaps worse—are derailed into failing or dropping out of school entirely.

Before students read this essay, consider holding a discussion on the idea of tracking and the differences between homogeneous and heterogeneous grouping. At present, the movement in education seems to be towards heterogeneous grouping, but practices differ from classroom to classroom, and opinions vary among educators, parents, and teachers. Ironically, though, students are seldom asked which process they see as most beneficial.

Not only does Rose come up against a system that failed to recognize him as an individual, but he also comes up against a variety of teachers, most of whom—at least while he is in the "low" track—hinder rather than help him.

- Brother Dill: "troubled and unstable . . . he would lose control and shake or smack us."
- Phys. Ed. teacher: a jock who enjoyed humiliating his students, who made ethnic jokes and used gutter language.
- Mr. Mitropetros: had students read one play over and over since he had "little training in English."
- Mr. Montez: "tiny, soft-spoken and delicate." Had little authority and couldn't control the class.
- Brother Clint: the exception—"he was young and powerful and handsome"; discovers the error in Rose's tracking.

Consider the differences between these teachers (except for Brother Clint) and Jack MacFarland, whom Rose encounters only after the tracking error had been corrected.

- Jack MacFarland: taught "his heart out"; had his students working, reading, writing constantly; delivered "crafted" lectures, asked pertinent questions, wrote important information on the board, addressed the classics as well as modern literature; "the man immersed us in language," and he was intelligent, in control, and had goals and respect for his students.

Clearly these examples run the gamut of worst to best teachers. Students should feel free to discuss how many of their teachers were as bad or as dangerous as Brother Dill or as incredibly inspiring as Jack MacFarland.

Rose admits that once he was placed in appropriate-level classes, he had trouble keeping up. He didn't know how to study, and much of his success depended on mastering concepts that were not addressed in his previous courses. The "game," of course, is to work hard, to try, to persevere and not to give up. This set of rules was never mentioned by anyone at his previous level. Here, Rose brings in another piece of the learning puzzle. Teacher and methods are important to learning, but equally important is the student's understanding of what is expected and of being motivated to meet those expectations.

The Extended Thinking and Research activities suggested at the end of this piece would certainly work well as individual research projects. Both would also work as group debate projects. Students could debate both sides of the issue on grades: Should the college or university they are currently attending give grades or not? They can also do the same with the tracking issue. Should students be tracked in college (or grade school, high school) or not? Experience, research, facts, statistics, and testimonies should form the basis for ideas and opinions expressed during these debates.

Nicholas Gage, The Teacher Who Changed My Life (p. 188)
(Cross-Chapter Connections: "Arriving," "American Dreams and Creations")

Just as Mike Rose (text p. 176) credits a teacher with coming along at just the right time in his life, so, too, does Gage pay homage to a remarkable woman who made all the difference in his life. By comparing the mentors in these two pieces, students should come to see that there is no exact formula, no one way to teach. What matters most, they might conclude, for a productive student/mentor relationship, is that both the teacher and the student be willing to work hard and to care about the learning process as well as the end product.

While Gage credits Miss Hurd with much of his accomplishment, students should also recognize that other factors worked to make him ready and eager to learn (Question No. 1). Early in his life, Gage almost certainly discovered the importance of education from his mother (par. 15). For instance, readers can reasonably infer that he developed his love of reading at least partially from his mother's response to her own arduous fight for the right to learn to read. In addition, before he met Miss Hurd, he had already endured four years in a class for the mentally retarded (par. 4), so that by the time he was in a standard classroom, he was ready and eager to learn what the other children knew. He was ready, as Miss Hurd announced, to "work (his) tail off." Finally, in seventh grade Gage found an essential weapon that enabled him to develop as a writer: He found the courage to write from his heart.

Miss Hurd encourages her class to write about what they know from their own experiences. (You may remind your students that Raymond Carver's father [text p. 129] gave his son this same advice.) Some students may feel that seventh graders would be reluctant to write about themselves; others may feel just the opposite. Many educators agree that the early teen years are a time when most people are ego-centered. If the teacher can provide useful direction and, most important, establish trust, the majority of junior high students talk and write willingly about themselves. Like Gage, however, they are not necessarily eager to have everyone read what they write. In publishing Gage's essay, Miss Hurd took a risk that some students may find objectionable. Gage's defense of his mentor would probably be that she was an experienced teacher who knew two things: (1) the essay was exceptional, so few, if any, of Gage's peers would respond negatively; (2) a magical pride and self-esteem often come when a student sees his or her name in print.

You may want to encourage your students to experience this same feeling of pride by asking them all to publish at least one piece of writing during this semester. Initially, many students will groan, mumble, and complain that they could never achieve such a goal. However, writing letters to the editor or opinion columns for the school newspaper is an almost certain way for students to get published. Small local papers (perhaps in towns near your institution or students' home towns) are often more than willing to publish letters responding to an article or editorial. As an alternative, consider "publishing" sections of students' writings by photocopying and handing them out on a regular basis during the semester.

Questions No. 4 and 5 ask the students to think about Gage's experience in terms of their own lives. Students could respond to No. 4 by writing a poem about one particular season. They could also search through poetry anthologies to find poems in which the author connects a season with an emotion or an event.

As many other writers have done thus far, Gage uses an especially apt metaphor to describe Miss Hurd. He calls her a "catalyst" in his life. Literally, a catalyst is the agent that puts energy into motion and gets a process moving. Without a catalyst, little progress can be made, few changes can happen. Certainly students can come up with other metaphors that explain the role of a good teacher. You might also ask them to create an equally effective metaphor for the good student.

Grace Paley, The Loudest Voice (p. 194)
(Cross-Chapter Connections: "American Dreams and Creations," "Crossing Borders")

All of the authors thus far in this section have, in one way or another, recalled both the voices that educated them in a negative way and the voices that educated them in a positive way. In this short story, Paley focuses on the various voices within her two learning places: her home culture and her school environment. Ask students to consider how who we listen to affects who we are. Many of us seldom stop to think that we can choose those voices we wish to listen to. Shirley, however, does make such choices, and her creative amalgam of the voices she hears suggests how such selectivity can enable each of us to develop a humanly—and humanely—educated self.

What type of a character is Shirley Abramowitz? From reading the first paragraph alone, what do students know about her? They'll have to draw inferences in order to see that Shirley is an observant listener and an honest person ("My voice was the loudest").

In addition to this, as the next few paragraphs reveal, she is also a talker, a person who enjoys her own company, and enjoys the details of the world around her. Furthermore, she cares little about what other people think: She says that even when others tell her to be quiet, she still sings inside (par. 8). She is also a born director and a good organizer, as suggested by her rehearsal duties.

The first three questions spin off of Shirley's character and ask students to think of what they were like in sixth grade. Consider actually setting up a comparison between "Then" and "Now" to help students see what they have gained or lost since sixth grade. Using a diagram will facilitate this exercise. This example suggests possibilities, but should not limit students as they create their own chart.

Comparisons and Contrasts: Sixth Grade/Present		
Qualities to be compared	THEN	NOW
PHYSICAL APPEARANCE		
ATTITUDE TOWARD SCHOOL		
PERSONAL FREEDOM		
RELIGIOUS BELIEFS		
(AND SO ON)		

After students have worked on these lists, you may want to have them use the similarities and differences they have discovered as the basis for a journal entry or a brief in-class writing.

While Shirley remains the center of this story, the real conflict swirls around her, as her parents take sides on whether or not a Jewish girl should be in a traditional Christmas play. Both parents make good points. The father encourages Shirley because he feels that playing her role is one way to learn about the Christian culture. He believes that reading from the New Testament story of Christ's birth will teach Shirley about the beliefs of others without undermining her own Jewish beliefs. Shirley's mother, however (as well as several other members of the Jewish community), feels that the school has shown her and her culture disrespect by asking Shirley to play the role. To the mother, it is a role that disregards Shirley's religious and cultural beliefs.

You can promote discussion by asking students to suggest real-life dilemmas that parallel Shirley's situation. They may suggest controversies such as prayer in public places or flag salutations in school. In many towns across America, the Christmas crèche in a public place is also a point of controversy.

To the Jewish people in this story, the Christmas tree on the corner, which had been decorated with public funds, was disrespectful because it celebrated (in part, with their tax dollars) a holiday from another religious tradition. Shirley, however, looks on the tree with pity, since it "was a stranger in Egypt"—a Christian symbol in a Jewish neighborhood. As she listens to the voices around her, Shirley develops her own sense of truth; she does not feel the need to see the world exactly as do any of her "teachers" (from school, family, or neighborhood). As a matter of fact, from her part in the Christmas play, she begins to see the Christian version of Christmas as "lonesome" (Question No. 9). Perhaps she sees Christians as lonesome because she believes them to stand outside the warm, busy, richly verbal world in which she and her family live.

While Shirley's voice booms from the stage, her mother sits in the audience, embarrassed. Even though she disagrees with the part her daughter has accepted, she comes because she knows Shirley is proud of her part and of her strong voice. She puts aside her own doubts and objections and comes because she loves her daughter. As she watches, she thinks of the irony that the Christian children do not have the central roles. Mr. Hilton, the play director, thinks primarily about putting on a good play. As he assigns roles, he does not consider the children's beliefs; instead, he seeks out strong voices and lively personalities. His attitude seems to reinforce what Mrs. Abramowitz feels about Christmas in America: It is a celebration based on glittery appearances, but lacking in religious depth.

The Extended Thinking suggestions allow students to take a creative approach to the story by becoming a different character. They may also argue about how individual rights relate to religious ceremonies, or finally, they may take an objective approach to this topic by researching the practices and celebrations of other religions.

Anna Lee Walters, A Teacher Taught Me (p. 200)
(Cross-Chapter Connections: "Rights and Responsibilities," "Crossing Borders")

Unfortunately, our perceptions about different cultures and peoples are often slanted, depending upon the sources from which we obtain our knowledge. Possible sources include parents, friends, media, publications, teachers, and textbooks. The prereading questions raise an interesting issue for students; if they respond honestly, many will discover that what they learned about Native Americans in school was limited to the tradition of the first Thanksgiving and Custer's last stand. Through both of these incidents, we see extreme stereotypes: Native Americans are either totally generous and loving or totally savage and unfeeling. This insight provides a good opportunity to raise the issue of what are thought of as "positive" stereotypes. Are they as dangerous as negative stereotypes? Why?

In this poem, the Indian speaker reacts to several different encounters in school and suggests how these encounters forced her to look outside the education system to develop a sense of self. To help students respond to the topics that follow this poem, consider raising a few questions that lead them to draw their own inferences.

For example, what does a pat on the head generally mean? The pat can be affectionate or it can be a gesture of pity—as in "you poor little thing." In this poem, perhaps the teacher is reacting out of both pity and guilt. Is that how any student wants to be treated, especially in a classroom of her peers (Question No. 1)?

What is suggested by the speaker's holding words in her hand? Some may see a sense of empowerment, a sense of action. Yet as the speaker holds on to these words, instead of hands reaching out, we see the image of a clenched fist, a symbol of anger as well as frustration. The student holds on to this anger and frustration, saving it for just the right moment. As she goes through her school years, she holds on to other words—words like "squaw" from a "no color" boy.

She will finally let go of her teacher's pity and the boy's prejudice when, perhaps, she has a sense of who she is or when she has a sense of what the truth really is. The teacher seems well-meaning, yet condescending; she wants to "save the Indians," but all the speaker wants is a chance to be seen as an individual. What she learns in school is that no one has ever bothered to get beneath the surface of who she is or of what Native Americans are all about. That's what a teacher taught her.

SECTION THREE
WRITING TO EXPLAIN

READINGS: ROOTS AND MEMORIES

Photographs and Previews (pp. 220–222)
Suggestions for Writing

Photographs
1. From details in this photograph, can you tell in which country this picture was taken?

    What are the most obvious differences between this photograph and the photograph on the page opposite? Based on your findings, what conclusions can you draw about private versus public ceremonies?

2. What does this family's activity tell you about their beliefs and values?

    From the expression on the little girl's face in this scene, what do you imagine she is feeling?

3. Food is often an integral part of a traditional celebration. After looking carefully at this photo, describe what other elements play an important part in a traditional celebration.

    From the expressions on the family members' faces, do you conclude that this occasion is mainly a time for celebration or a time for reflection?

Previews
1. From these quotations, what would you say is at the root of how each individual perceives the world?

2. According you these quotations, what might most of us need to do in order to get a sense of who we are?

Cross-Reference List: Alternative Selections for "Roots and Memories"

Selection	Text Page
All Selections in "Arrivals"	36–99
All Selections in "Parents and Children"	100–146
All Selections in "Ways of Learning"	148–202
Quilts and Women's Culture	331
Everyday Use (fiction)	337
Where I Come from Is Like This	351
Between a Rock and a Soft Place: A Century of American Manhood	359
Lullaby (fiction)	484
A Question of Language	520
Don't Let Them Chip Away at Our Language (poem)	551
The Trip Back (fiction)	600
What Were They Like? (poem)	611

Toni Morrison, *from* **The Site of Memory** (p. 223)
(Cross-Chapter Connections: "Parents and Children," "Ways of Learning")

Morrison's essay vividly describes events and people in her life and, in addition, explains the significance of these events and people. The two prereading questions encourage students to follow a similar process of analysis by asking them to explain why they think a certain memory has stayed with them or why they wrote in the past.

Moving from "what" to "why" encourages critical thinking. During class discussions, for instance, you may find it helpful to keep returning to the question "Why?" If a student is willing, you may use the first prereading response to show the class just how "deep" the "whys" can take us:

Q: Why did you focus on the memory of caramels?

A: Because my grandmother made them for us at Christmas.

Q: But why do you think of your grandmother?

A: Because I was really close to her.

Q: Why?

A: I don't know. . . . She was always someone I looked up to.

Q: Why?

A: Well, I guess because she had such a good attitude. Even when she was ninety years old, she would sing and dance— as much as she could with her cane. And her eyes still saw everything, sometimes even what you thought.

Q: Why do you think she was different from other old people?

A: She once told me, "The only time I'm unhappy is when I don't have enough to do. So remember to always have something to do each day, something planned. That way you'll never get lonely."

As you can see from this sequence, the student has moved from the initial image of "caramels" to a deeper understanding of what her grandmother was all about. She knows now why the caramels are important. They are the symbol of her grandmother's keeping busy, staying happy.

Seeking to discover "why" allows Morrison to get in touch with her own writing process and to understand why she writes about the things she does. For example, she starts with an image of Hannah and ends up thinking about friendship between women. This "world of women" (Question No. 1) comprises the silent understanding women have of the deep parts of one another's lives—the hopes, the fears, the regrets, the losses, the possibilities, the dreams. Students often find it easier to share their responses to Morrison's question in small groups, rather than in a whole-class discussion. In addition, small groups allow more time for students to ask each other "why" they have made a particular observation.

To answer her own "whys," Morrison goes back to images in her childhood. Most students will see Morrison's childhood as filled with strong relationships. Her parents were close, as were she and her sister. In going back to her family, she envisions the image of corn. By asking herself why, she recognizes that she associates corn with a life filled with friends, family, and freedom.

In her book for reluctant writers, *Writing Down the Bones*, Natalie Goldberg tells her readers that when they absolutely have nothing they want to write about, they should just write about food: a favorite food, an unusual food, the food they dislike the most, the food they feel is most like them. Such a strategy really works (as Morrison proves), for when it comes to food, people are usually eager to talk—and write! Most students won't mind writing about their own favorite foods, and they'll be eager to share these observations as well.

As far as Morrison's own process goes (Question No. 5), students may have to read between the lines to understand her philosophy and process of writing. Perhaps if you phrase questions for students, they can come to a fuller view of Morrison's process and their own as well:

- What would Morrison say a writer should write about?
  (Anything he or she knows, something that reveals the truth, something that perhaps starts with an image and moves to a deeper level of understanding for both the reader and the writer.)
- What should a writer aim to do?
  (To explore "the actual and the possible"—to hold the reader's attention, to keep mystery and truth somehow side by side.)
- What's the most important thing a writer should do before writing?
  (Observe the details within the exterior and interior worlds, to raise questions about these observations, and to distinguish which of the questions are the most valuable to explore—and to remember what really was and what might have been.)

The tools a writer needs, then, would include some of the following: an imagination, a memory, an observant eye, a curious spirit, a willingness to question, an openness to explore possibilities, the courage to remember, the courage to tell the truth, the courage to withhold the truth, discipline, dedication, a wish to give something back to the world (Question No. 7).

Now that they have been immersed in Morrison's writing process as well as their own, you might ask them to explore the processes of their favorite authors. In addition, suggest that copying passages from this author's works will immerse the student into a product as well as the process. Initially, students may not see the usefulness of such an exercise (Extended Thinking and Research suggestion No. 2). You might point out that copying is a time-honored tool for developing a vocabulary of style and for understanding the nature of the choices all writers have. In the end, such exercises often enable students to explain "why" they like or dislike a certain author—and this step moves them from being readers who are responding to becoming readers who are evaluating and assessing.

Clearly, to Morrison the process of discovery while writing is more important than the product of the writing (Question No. 6). The rigorous sense of growth and change that comes during writing is often more energizing than the pride and satisfaction that comes when it's finished. Students can perhaps understand this concept if you relate it to similar processes: dancing, painting, weaving, sketching, running, singing, playing an instrument, competing in sports, and so forth.

Charlene Spretnak, Ecofeminism: Our Roots and Flowering (p. 228) (Cross-Chapter Connections: "Men and Women," "Rights and Responsibilities")

Charlene Spretnak's essay explains and analyzes historical information. This complex process makes this essay one of the most difficult pieces in this text for many students. Those who can be encouraged to read and reread, without losing heart, will discover a thoughtful historical and philosophical approach to understanding modern women's roles, rights, and responsibilities.

The prereading questions move students to consider their own experiences in connection with the world. Most students are eager to explain what they believe are the three greatest problems facing the world. They may also relish a hearty debate on the third question. When they've explored their own ideas on nature and the world's problems, they may find Spretnak's ideas a bit more accessible.

For example, Spretnak passionately urges respect for the balance in nature and explains how completely the existence of our world depends upon this natural order and balance (par. 1). Students will find Spretnak's ideas relating to the United States primarily in the following paragraphs: 2, 3, 15, 16, 17, 18, 22, 26. The motif of women's connection with the world of nature permeates this piece. Specifically, students can cite main ideas from the following paragraphs: 4, 11, 13, 14, 15, 23.

Since many of the paragraphs in this essay are relatively long, you may want students to write a one-sentence summary of those paragraphs they (or you) deem most complex. Comparing sentence summaries provides a possible way for students to better understand Spretnak's main points. After students have summarized each paragraph, they are ready to write a one-page summary of the essay. Before they do so, ask them to try writing a one-sentence summary of the whole piece. To do this, they have to recognize the main images: women, nature, ecology, spirituality, world, action. From here, they can construct a sentence to focus their individual summaries.

Spretnak's article could certainly appeal to diverse groups of men and women, such as historians, scientists, or philosophers. However, women are almost certainly her main audience. Considering the sophistication of her text, students should be more specific, going beyond the identification of gender and/or professional background: For instance, what age group or groups would be most interested? What might be their educational background? Their philosophical, political, or religious beliefs?

Asking students to define *ecofeminism* moves them to the heart of this essay. Basically, the term refers to a movement of women who share a connectedness with nature and who work to improve the relationship of humans with the earth and with one another. Spretnak's definition does not necessarily imply that men are not concerned with nature or with the world's problems. For example, in paragraph 9 she refers to the men who discovered ecofeminism while exploring environmental problems. She does, however, claim that, traditionally, women have been healers, while men have been controllers (Question No. 3).

The essay's organization enables readers to find the specific roots that led to the development of ecofeminism. Beginning with paragraph 5, Spretnak introduces "the many paths":

- The women's movement in the 1960s
- Marxist analysis and the dominance theory
- Nature-based religions that uphold the Goddess theory
- Environmentalism

Students should think about how these paths connect to the ecofeminism movement. What basic tenets relate the Goddess theory and ecofeminism? Students may recognize offshoots from these paths as well—such as the current women's movement's impact in the workplace, for example, or scientific advances that substantiate environmental problems. Political unrest also provides a path that leads women to be more concerned, more protective of their families and their world (Question No. 4).

The garden metaphor reveals the interconnectedness of all people and this world. Certainly Spretnak sees us all as a part of this garden, the world. If we take care of this garden, the flowers and plants will grow and prosper. Our roots will grow strong and our petals will be colorful. However, if we fail to nurture this garden, if we allow technology to trample on it at will, we will have nothing left but a wasteland. A garden depends on cooperation and balance. Spretnak calls for all women to "seek intimate communion with the natural world."

If you want students to develop their own images of America today, have them contemplate the following phrase:

> Today, America is like a(n) . . .

As an alternative exercise, you may want them to focus on a particular aspect of the environment. For example:

> Today, Lake Superior (or Boston Harbor or the Great Salt
> Lake or Yellowstone Park, and so on) is like a(n) . . .

Questions number 6 and 9 are related since both ask students to give their own assessments of the modern world and to suggest specific actions that may help people to be more connected with nature. As students evaluate the relationships between men and women, they should be able to give specific examples to support their opinions. The actions, as well, should be specific. For example, instead of saying, "We should all recycle," students should be able to explain why that action would help people "seek intimate communion with the natural world" (or any other specific quotation from this question).

Ecophilosophy technically is a belief in the importance of maintaining a healthy balance in the natural environment. In order to write a more detailed definition, students should aim to include one or more of the following in their answers:

- an example
- an illustration
- a comparison/contrast (what it is like, what it is not)
- a cause and an effect
- subgroups within this term

Before students paraphrase paragraph 23, explain that short paragraphs can be effective in certain situations. For example, you might note that a writer may use a paragraph with only one or two sentences as a transition between two major ideas. Before students begin writing, remind them to use only their own words. Have students read one sentence, flip the page over, and then write the thought entirely in their own words. Such paraphrasing may go something like this:

> This movement of women for the universe will continue because we will always care and connect with one another. This connection is the source of our energy and provides the meaning of our lives. We must discover how to put this modern world into perspective so that respect for one another and nature becomes and remains our focus.

After reading and discussing this essay both orally and in writing, students have several options. They can evaluate whether or not this essay would be effective for readers of their local newspapers; they can research and compare religions as well as authors; they can write an essay in which they support Spretnak's ideas or challenge them. As one of the most demanding essays in this book, "Ecofeminism" challenges students to think and write on a rigorous academic level.

Adrienne Rich, Split at the Root (p. 239)
(Cross-Chapter Connections: "American Dreams and Creations," "Crossing Borders," "Ways of Learning")

The basic question Rich raises in this essay should connect to each and every student in your class: "Who am I, really?" The prereading questions encourage students to think about what is important to them, what they're most concerned with at this point in their lives, and who they really are. Although topic No. 3 is really meant as a warm-up or brainstorming exercise, it provides a fine opportunity for analyzing by asking students to look at parts to determine the meaning of the whole. Clearly the one- to two-sentence analysis is really the difficult part of this exercise.

Students move to thinking about the essay as well when they are asked to identify not only what an author includes, but also what she omits. In paragraph 6, Rich gives the following details of her birthplace:

- Baltimore
- hospital in black ghetto—her father worked there
- white marble statue of Christ in the lobby

Now why would she include these specific details? (You may want to remind students that Rich is a poet and ask them in what ways her writing suggests poetry. Possibilities include her fine eye for details and the way she inspires readers to read between, above, and beyond the lines.)

Students may see that Baltimore is a major American city, in a state that is caught, in some ways, between the North and the South. The hospital in a black ghetto reflects that she, who is white, was born among black people, so here she was the "outsider." As a prestigious researcher, her father also may have felt like an outsider in the neighborhood where the hospital is located. The hospital itself, perhaps, is symbolic of that which is socially acceptable, while the white marble statue stands in direct contrast to poor, urban conditions. The statue of Christ, of course, stands in contrast to Rich's Jewish heritage. In just these three everyday details students can see a whole complexity of relationships at work.

The souvenirs from Rich's grandfather (par. 7) provide the reader with more insights that relate directly to the author herself. Readers are invited to consider the significance of these souvenirs: an ivory flute, a thin gold pocket watch, and a Hebrew prayer book. You'll need to call on all your skills to enable students who can't seem to get beyond the literal to think more fully and deeply. Here are some possibilities:

- ivory flute: valuable, fine material, made for carrying; instrument can be a sign of harmony or of cacophony. An instrument has little meaning by itself. Only when it is played, when the breath of the player rushes through, can it realize full potential.
- thin gold pocket watch: slender, fragile, valuable, placed next to the heart, keeping time, moving forward.
- Hebrew prayer book: Jewish heritage, support from God, a book whose many pages are centered on one purpose.

To synthesize these meanings, Rich searches for harmony and meaning in her life. She values the truth as she looks for who she is, and examining time—both past and present—has contributed to her quest.

In paragraph 8, Rich explains why her father doesn't talk about his Jewish ancestry. As an outsider in the South, he probably did not want his children to feel the loneliness and prejudice he had suffered. His Jewish heritage may have been more of a burden to him than a cause for celebration (Question No. 3).

Again, the Southern culture comes into play when Rich talks about "white social Christianity." As Rich observed the practice of Christianity in her community, she saw it as primarily a social activity in which the wealthier, white people engaged. For these people, religious values included ideals and manners, but not necessarily compassion or truth (par. 14–20).

A primary danger, of course, in "flirting with identity" (Question No. 5) is that one's discoveries will destroy familiar, comfortable images. Trying on new identities often requires betraying or discarding a former self. Thus, when Rich began learning about Judaism, she was bound to either accept it or reject it; when she began searching for her sexual identity, she had to either accept a heterosexual lifestyle or deny it.

Rich examines the stereotypical notions of being Jewish in paragraphs 30–34. When she speaks about the "wrong kind of Jew," she is not, herself, casting aspersions. Since she puts this phrase in quotation marks, she indicates that she is giving the "white social Christian image" of the "wrong kind" of Jew (par. 35). This "stereotype" was everything she was brought up not to be: loud, aggressive, successful, intelligent, self-righteous.

When Rich talks about the various parts of herself, she is really explaining who she is and and analyzing how a combination of cultures provided an amazing variety of ingredients (par. 39). What happens when people lose their culture (Question No. 7)? To encourage students to struggle with this question, have them go back to prereading topic No. 3 which asks them to write, in five different completions of the same sentence, who they are. What would happen if they had to eliminate any one of their answers? What would they lose? What might they gain?

To demonstrate, you could list your own responses on the board. Example: Who Am I?

Teacher

Mother

Writer

Sister

Wife

Or:

Researcher

Feminist

Democrat

Catholic

Franco-American

If any of the above were eliminated, what would be changed? Clearly, any one part that disappears affects the whole. Something dies, and with it a whole branch of possibilities and understandings comes to an end.

Whether or not a person has to profess openly the beliefs of a culture for that culture to remain important in his or her life is up for discussion. In Rich's own story, her father did not talk openly about his Jewish heritage, and yet Rich pursued it. However, he did talk about Judaism enough to give her some sense of his beliefs.

The Extended Thinking and Research suggestions invite students to explore the meanings of the qualities they value (courage, identity, and so forth) as well as the values and ideas suggested by any of Rich's poetry they choose. In response to complaints from some students that these topics lead to more questions than answers, Rich would probably observe that questioning provides the best means for growth.

Mark Mathabane, The African Contribution (p. 250)
(Cross-Chapter Connections: "Ways of Learning," "Crossing Borders")

While Adrienne Rich (text p. 239) explores her sense of self through memories and rebellion, and Jay Ford (text p. 257) achieves a new understanding of his own identity through immersing himself in another culture, Mathabane recognizes a fuller view of who he is by connecting to the literature of black American authors. Students who have read "Learning to Read and Write" by Frederick Douglass (text p. 151) will recognize similarities in the way these two men evaluate the power of reading to change their lives.

The prereading questions ask students to reflect on one of their favorite books. They are also asked to think about their approach to learning something new so they can put themselves in Mathabane's shoes as he comes to terms with discovering how to write about himself. (You may want to refer students to Morrison's "Site of Memory" [text p. 223] to compare the writing process.)

Undoubtedly, Mathabane will seem like an extraordinary learner to some students. For example, in his free time, he browses in the library and then finds a book he can't put down. Of course, his real learning is due in part to his passion for the topic—he just can't seem to get enough of these writers. He is so caught up with these writers' ideas because, as a native of South Africa, he has seen his own people experience the pains and injustices of segregation and racial prejudice (Question No. 2).

To initiate discussion, ask students to list topics they feel they could read about extensively without getting bored. Such topics may provide resources for future papers or research projects.

Mathabane sets out on a zealous quest to learn to write as effectively as the writers who inspired him, for as he says, he wanted "to purge myself of what they had purged themselves of so eloquently." He is inspired because the writers made a profound difference in his life, and he realizes that he, too, can make a profound difference if he can write so well (Question No. 3). For him, writing now has a purpose. If students think about writing they have done when they had a specific purpose and destiny, they may be able to identify with Mathabane's ambitious goal.

As he strives to write profoundly, Mathabane discovers that writing from one's own passion and experience is far more effective than trying to adopt someone else's language and style. He also has the good sense to look thoughtfully at what other writers have to say about writing. What he discovers is that most good writers read a great deal. They also care passionately about the subjects they explore. Like Mathabane, the authors he admired were driven to share their writing with others.

As he continues his education, Mathabane reads some of the world's greatest philosophers, and once again, his eyes are opened to injustice. He becomes obsessed with the world of ideas. Many traditional-age freshmen may not have experienced this immersion in ideas that challenge them to think and question all that they once knew. However, you may ask them what ideas they have explored so far in college that have intrigued them. You may also ask them to think about how their ideas and beliefs have changed in any way since they have come to school (Question No. 6).

Mathabane feels as if his awakening is happening at a time in America when many students have settled into a kind of malaise. He compares their attitudes with the social activism and consciousness exemplified by the demonstrations and protests of the late 1960s and early 1970s, when campuses were alive with ideals and ideas. As students think back on this time in history, you may ask them to respond, in writing, to the following quotation from Allan Bloom's book, *Closing of the American Mind:*

> Students these days are nice. I choose this word carefully.
> They are not, however, particularly noble or moral.

This quotation is guaranteed to set off a variety of emotions—from anger to sadness to self-righteousness.

When students read the poem, encourage them to try to see it as a movie or a set of photos. Responses to what they learned about Africa and Mathabane may mention how full of life and idealism both the author and his view of Africa are. They may also realize that the emotions he feels for his childhood are quite similar to feelings many of us have about our early lives.

Extended Thinking and Research topics allow students to pursue the path that intrigues them the most. Do they want to know more about South African politics? Do they, like Mathabane, want to research the lives and processes of their favorite authors? Would they like to discover the world and ideas of black authors? Do they want to read the works of authors who speak to them of their own ancestors and cultures? One of these paths may lead at least a few students to a sense of discovery and intense commitment similar to Mathabane's.

Jay Ford, 20/20 Hindsight (p. 257)
(Cross-Chapter Connections: "Ways of Learning," "Crossing Borders")

Like Rich, Jay Ford goes on a journey to discover more about his culture. While Rich journeys through memories, Ford travels physically to a different culture where he discovers new insights about himself. To prepare for reading this essay, students can write about an imagined excursion to Africa. In addition, they might think, through writing or discussion, about a time when they were in a minority. Remind students they can be in a minority based on many criteria other than race, religion, gender, or national origin. For example, they may be in a minority because of their thoughts, beliefs, and actions, or, perhaps because of the perceived status of the work they are doing (many students have been employed as waiters, fast-food workers, clerks, bell-hops and have held other service-oriented jobs where customers—and supervisors—may treat them with little respect or personal regard).

Initially, Ford believes that Kenya is just like the United States. He sees the city of Nairobi as much like any American city—tall buildings, traffic, businesses, and so forth. However, when he observes more astutely, he notices the subtle differences. From this initial lesson, Ford recognizes that to know something, one has to look carefully—and more than once (Question No. 1).

The second question connects well with the third prereading topic. What does it feel like to be a minority? By offering their own experiences and by writing on this question, students should be able to either support or question Ford's observations that those in the minority often feel inferior and insecure.

Ford realizes that to be accepted into this culture, he has to become one with the language and one with the customs and manners of the culture (Question No. 3). You may want students to discuss exactly what it means to "assimilate," and how or whether that term differs from "accommodate." In addition, students should think about the similarities and differences between the treatment the Kenyans accorded Ford and the treatment they might typically give a visitor from another country. Would most of them open their doors? Would most Americans? (There should be examples from both sides to this question.) Would they, as Kenyans did, "welcome foreigners for an unlimited number of days"?

Perhaps students will see that many of the differences come from expectations and values. Americans are used to their own homes and yards. They value their individual rights and their privacy. Ford terms this lifestyle as "linear." Americans tend to depend on order and consistency, he writes. Ask for students' reactions to the differences in lifestyles described in paragraphs 15–17. Do they think Americans are "linear," and if so, is this a lifestyle they would prefer over the more chaotic course in Kenya (Questions 5 and 6)? Might some prefer a modification—for instance, a primarily linear lifestyle that, nonetheless, embraced and even sought chaos from time to time. Examples would be welcome here.

Students should think about Ford's contention that Americans are more concerned with material goods than they are with one another. You might initiate the assessment by asking students to write briefly on the following question:

> If you were going away for one year, what would you take with you? (Limit your list to three choices.)

Students who list, for example, photographs of people or address books or stationery challenge Ford's assumptions. Those who would take cars, stereos, and jewelry may confirm his views.

Students can also find cause to argue or support Ford's vision of American education (Question No. 8). Do students go to school to learn? If so, have them give examples. If not, have students explain why Americans go to school. Ask them to think back on students with whom they went to school as well as on their own classroom experiences and motivations.

Ford writes to explain and praise the culture and people in Kenya. Is he also trying to bridge the gap between America and Kenya, or does he make the gap wider? Is he trying to get Americans to change in some way? From his ending, it would seem as if he is trying to show that the world is an enormous place and that by assimilating into another culture, at least for a while, one becomes a wiser person (Question No. 9).

Students may disagree with some of the points in this comparison (Ford's assessment of American values and lifestyles), but they should be able to see what Ford learned by daring to experience the back roads of another culture. (Students can add their own experiences to Ford's if they choose to do the second and third Extended Thinking suggestions.) You may also want to have students read "On a Greek Holiday" by Alice Bloom (text p. 559), for she, too, promotes the notion of becoming one with a foreign culture and critiques what she defines as the typical American view of foreign experience.

David Morris, Rootlessness (p. 265)
(Cross-Chapter Connections: "American Dreams and Creations")

David Morris asks students to consider the following question: Do Americans today have the sense of security and community that they did prior to 1960? To get students thinking in terms of this past society, the prereading questions invite students to compare aspects of their present lives with the same aspects of their lives in the past.

Contrasting their own early years with their current lives leads students to Morris's essay, which juxtaposes past and present views of American neighborhoods. Although, as Morris acknowledges, Americans have always been known for their restlessness, he believes that since the 1950s, the spirit of community and of being settled within American neighborhoods has been decreasing. He sees this alienation as resulting from four primary forces: government urban renewal projects, the economics of the "mall mentality," zoning laws, and America's overreliance on the car (Question No. 1).

To assess the differences Morris identifies, students could compare their neighborhoods during their growing-up years to what they are like now. Are we more disconnected now because of the change in neighborhoods? Might other social forces come into play as well— forces like the advent of cable television and home computers?

So what if the neighborhood bar has disappeared? Does it make a difference? If students think back to a place they used to go (a corner market, a neighborhood park, a local pub), can they verbalize what they miss most of all? Those who agree with Morris may come to the conclusion that what they miss is a sense of belonging, of familiarity. If so, where can they go now to have this same feeling?

Morris strongly believes in rebuilding communities to enhance a sense of camaraderie and closeness. Students should examine each one of his ideas (par. 17–23) to see whether they would work in their own towns or cities. For example, Morris says that if we impose a monthly fee for using cars, people may start walking more. Do students think this is true? Why or why not? Morris also says that the United States should prohibit takeovers from competitive outsiders. Should the United States prohibit, say, German or Swiss or Japanese investors from buying local businesses? Promoting small business is another idea Morris believes will unite the community. At present, the trend is for larger businesses to swallow up small companies. Should legislation be passed to make such take-overs difficult or even illegal? Are Morris's ideas practical? Are they desirable? Are they merely idealistic dreams? (Question No. 5)

Students may realize that Morris almost certainly wants this piece of writing to make a difference. His tone suggests that he believes deeply in the sense of community, and he sees this concept as basic to America's future. His descriptions of "small town America" versus the way things are now would certainly appeal to readers who grew up in close, connected neighborhoods as well as to readers who believe in the importance of returning to what they see as the simpler values and lifestyles of the past. On the other hand, those who value the mobility of our present society, as well as those who prefer privacy to group activity, may not be quite so responsive to Morris's ideas.

Students can continue with Morris's train of thought by exploring how other countries encourage community. They can also conduct interviews with people in their own neighborhoods to discover what changes have taken place during the past thirty years. In addition, they can put their observational skills to work by watching the interactions in a local mall or an older, downtown area.

Amy Tan, Two Kinds (p. 270)
(Cross-Chapter Connections: "Parents and Children," "American
Dreams and Creations")

In this reading, students meet two wonderful characters, yet they
also encounter the gaps that cultural differences can create even
between members of the same family. Most students can readily
identify with a culture gap. First of all, their peer culture is different
from their parents' (and, for older students, from their children's).
With each generation, values and preoccupations shift a bit, so if
students do some of the prereading exercises, they may be able to
recognize several different cultures that initiate conflict between Jing-
mei and her mother. Not only are they from different generations, but,
in addition. each has internalized values related to the land of her
birth—Jing-mei is American-born; her mother was born in China.

Many students will see Jing-mei's mother as a parent who
desperately wants her daughter to succeed in this new country. Some
may believe that she puts too much pressure on her daughter. Most
will also agree that the mother is caught between the Hollywood
version of America and her traditional Chinese values. One culture
says, "Succeed"; the other says, "Be content."

Many students will recognize in Jing-mei some of the conflicts
from their own childhoods. She wants to please her mother, yet she
also wants to be in control of her own life. In addition, she wants to do
well, but she doesn't necessarily want to put in the effort and discipline
needed to be better. In her struggle to be her own person, her stubborn
nature seems to be both her strength and her weakness.

In the beginning of the story, the mother and daughter seem to be
on the same wavelength: They both think that Jing-mei "would soon
become perfect." However, as soon as Jing-mei begins to have trouble
with her mother's tests, they begin to grow apart. As Jing-mei says, "I
hated the tests, the raised hopes and failed expectations." In turn, Jing-
mei becomes angry because she doesn't think her mother accepts her
for who she is—a less-than-perfect, ordinary young girl.

Tan is a powerful storyteller, and students can recognize her talent
by pointing to the words or events in the story that affect them the
most. The innocence and idealism Jing-mei and her mother both
demonstrate as they watch television shows, the inside workings of
Jing-mei's mind, the actions and hopes of her mother, the comic piano

lesson and the interactions between Jing-mei and her nearly deaf teacher—all swing the reader among various emotions: hope, antici- pation, anger, disappointment, humor, sorrow, acceptance.

Consider asking students to look for one quotation that affects them strongly. You might tell them that many successful writers have the habit of copying one quotation a day—either something they've heard or something they've read—as part of a resource journal. Often they include their own observations and responses to this quotation.

Old Chong is a wonderful character, one who certainly provides comic relief. He also is a symbolic character in this piece, especially because he is deaf. Similarly, Jing-mei is deaf to her mother's wisdom ("Who ask you to be genius? Only ask you be your best."), and the mother is deaf to her daughter's pleading ("Why don't you like me the way I am?").

The conflict reaches a climax when Jing-mei's mother wants her to resume practicing the piano, even after her disastrous concert. Some students may feel as if Jing-mei is justified in balking at her mother; others may feel as if the words the daughter uses are cruel and hurtful. Certainly, the mother is hurt for, as Tan writes, she went away "like a small brown leaf, then, brittle, lifeless," and the older Jing-mei, look- ing back, says "It also felt good, that this awful side of me had surfaced, at last."

When Jing-mei finally returns as an adult to claim, and play, her childhood piano, she sees things differently. The piano now sounds "richer than I remembered." She is also surprised at how well she can really play after all those years. Most of all, she recognizes that her mother did know her very well and did love her for who she was. Perhaps she just wanted her daughter to recognize how good she could be.

After students have read the story, the title may take on a new meaning as students think about this question in terms of both the daughter and the mother. As far as the daughter is concerned, she feels her mother represents two kinds of people: a loving, protective mother, yet a mother who is too demanding. The mother is caught between "two kinds" of America: the idealistic, movie version and the independent version. The music, too, as Jing-mei discovers in the moving conclusion, can be played in "two kinds" of styles: one is light and easy (like the daughter when she isn't pressured); the other is longer and faster (the more defiant and angry child, perhaps). In the end, Jing-mei recognizes that the two kinds are not entirely opposed. Each is part of a unified and harmonious whole; she need not deny the hopes and values of her Chinese-born mother to be true to the values she has absorbed growing up in America.

For further understanding, students can read Tan's *Joy Luck Club*, they can research in greater depth one Chinese tradition, or they can write their own view of either of the main characters in this piece. Students may also want to compare and contrast further the factors that unite and separate two people by reading Gish Jen's short story, "What Means Switch" in the "Questions of Language" chapter (text p. 536).

Lorna Dee Cervantes, Refugee Ship (p. 281)
(Cross-Chapter Connections: "Arriving," "Crossing Borders")

Students may have to read this poem several times before they fully experience the rhythm and feeling of this short piece. Reading the poem aloud makes it much easier to detect the back-and-forth motion that suggests the jolting of the waves. Consider reading the piece out loud for your class and then asking the students what the rhythm reminds them of.

To get students used to rereading a poem, you may ask them to read it through quickly and then jot down just one image that stays with them. Some students will see a face in a mirror, others will see a ship in the middle of the sea, and a few may see the first image: that of a young girl sneaking past her mother.

The simile "like wet cornstarch" is intriguing. Students may see this image as a sticky substance or a slippery one. Stickiness implies being unable to move, to progress from one spot to another; slippery indicates not being able to take hold in one spot. Either way, the simile works to reveal the dilemma in which the speaker finds herself as she is caught between two cultures.

The details in the mirror—the "brown skin, black hair"—reveal, of course, the speaker's concern with her heritage. She doesn't mention her eyes or her mouth, presumably because they do not seem distinctively related to her ethnic background.

The image of the ship that will never dock is stark and lonely. The ship belongs neither here nor there; it can only wait on the outside and watch. As it waits, it rocks, upsetting any people who may be on board. The repetition reinforces the despair the speaker feels. Perhaps the first line is one of sorrow, the other is one of anger, or vice versa. The repetition gives more emotion, more finality, to the place in which the speaker finds herself.

The poet's decision not to capitalize the word *Spanish* may suggest that the speaker sees the halfway position of the ship as reflecting the loss of distinct cultural values experienced by many immigrants. The country of their birth no longer seems like the customary, all-important place that a capitalized noun would suggest.

READINGS: AMERICAN DREAMS AND CREATIONS

Photographs and Previews (pp. 284–286)
Suggestions for Writing

Photographs

1. What "dream" might the dancers in this photograph be celebrating?

   In what way does the background of this piece contrast with the dancers? Why might this contrast be important to the theme of this scene?

2. What do you think this woman is thinking or feeling as she goes about her task of preparing the yarn?

   Are there any details in this photograph which do not support the notion of a Native American culture?

3. What's your first reaction after glancing at this photograph?

   From the people in this photograph, what conclusions can you draw about the effects that Elvis's life—and death—had on America?

Previews

1. Which one of these art forms—music, singing, weaving, acting, or writing—interests you the most? With which art form might you be the most uncomfortable?

2. From these quotes, would you say that art is meant to elevate life or to reflect it?

Cross-Reference List: Alternative Selections for "American Dreams and Creations"

Nitaya Kanchanawan, Elvis, Thailand, and I (p. 287)
(Cross-Chapter Connections: "Roots and Memories," "Crossing Borders")

To accompany Kanchanawan's evaluation of an American rock star's effect on her life in Thailand, consider bringing into the classroom either several videos of Elvis in action or recordings of several of his hit songs. While most students will be familiar with the 1950s star, these video or audio recordings will provide a common experience for the class and help students to connect more fully with the author's views.

Elvis's popularity in the United States has been attributed to a number of factors: He was the poor boy who never took formal music lessons, yet he made it to the top; he also introduced excitement and rebellion to a calm and quiet time in American history; and, of course, he was handsome and young, a movie star and a singer all in one. The Thai liked him for these reasons as well. Yet, Elvis's popularity in Thailand, according to Kanchanawan, had an additional, culturally based reason. He was greatly acclaimed for his polite and honest demeanor, which, the author notes, made him "just like a Thai" (Question No. 1).

From this essay, students may learn about Elvis, but they should also learn more about Thailand. Among other things, this essay investigates the implications of Thai pronunciations (par. 2), politics (par. 5, 15), culture (par. 8, 10), and preferences (par. 9, 14) (Question No. 2).

The effects of Elvis's music differ sharply between the United States and Thailand. Elvis changed music in America, and he introduced a sensual, rebellious image as a role model that shocked many parents just as it intrigued and delighted many American teens. However, in Thailand he had two different effects. First, "he provoked more interest in American popular music" (par. 5), and, more important, he gave Thailand an image of Americans as kind, caring, and polite (par. 10).

To support this view of Elvis, Kanchanawan points to the fact that Elvis supported his family (par. 10). Because of this fact alone, the Thais respected him. After Elvis's death, the Thais praised him for being so "devoted to his parents" (par. 14) and for being so generous with his money. As they saw it, Elvis shared their beliefs in the importance of family (Question No. 6).

Kanchanawan probably includes this information because, as far as the Thais were concerned, their impressions of most Americans were decidedly unfavorable. As she writes in paragraph 10, Americans were seen as disrespectful, uncaring, and rude. Perhaps this image of Americans was fostered by the media. You may ask students to think about the popular television shows in the late 1950s and early 1960s. How were Americans portrayed? Ask students, too, to research what America was like, according to newspapers and magazines, during this same time period. Following World War II and the Korean War, many saw the United States and its citizens as wealthy and powerful (Question No. 5 and 8).

Students can make their own comparisons as they discuss whether or not Americans today are able to express their emotions freely and openly (Question No. 4), offering specific examples (from life experiences or from media images) to support whichever viewpoint they take.

For the Thais, Elvis's image as a rebel was overshadowed by his image as a proponent of idealism and family values. In the time between Elvis's initial fame and his death, the world changed drastically. Ask students to list the events that come to mind when they think of the years between 1956, when Elvis had his first hit, and 1977, when he died. The following tragedies might be named: the assassinations of John Kennedy, Martin Luther King, Robert Kennedy; the Vietnam War; Watergate and Agnew's and Nixon's resignations, just to mention a few (Question No. 8).

Certainly, these events and others might have contributed to the less-than-honorable impression of the United States held by citizens of many countries worldwide. Thus, in the conclusion of her essay, Kanchanawan mentions how surprised Thais were to realize that Americans still remembered Elvis, even years after his death. This sentimental response seemed to them to contradict the image of cold, heartless Americans who killed their own leaders and engaged in controversial wars. For many Thais, Elvis, the hometown boy who took care of his parents and sang about love, reflected values quite different from what they saw as representative of mainstream America in the late 1970s (Question No. 8).

As a follow-up to this essay, students can examine a current American superstar, they can learn more about Elvis (to value, perhaps, the Thais' image of him), or they might learn about a superstar from another country, evaluating the reasons for his or her popularity within a given culture.

William Zinsser, Shanghai Blues (p. 293)
(Cross-Chapter Connections: "Ways of Learning," "Questions of Language," "Crossing Borders")

Diverse topics—including the history of jazz in America, the effect of Communism on Chinese artists, elements of good music, and the musical connections between two totally different cultures—come together to suggest intriguing contrasts and comparisons. Before students read William Zinsser's thought-provoking essay, consider allowing extra class time for listening to recordings of jazz musicians as well as of traditional Chinese music. If you know of any local musicians or if any students in your class are musicians, consider staging a live workshop so that students can observe, as well as ask questions of, a musician at work. Particularly important is the concept of improvisation, so natural to most American minds and spirits yet so strange and alien to the Chinese music students.

The three prereading questions serve to get students in touch with their own artistic processes as well as the processes and accomplishments of other artists. Thus, they should be ready to follow with interest and understanding the accomplishments and struggles of the musicians Zinsser introduces.

Before students answer the first discussion question, you may want to ask them to jot down their responses when they hear the word *jazz*. What do they already know about this musical form? In Ruff's opening talk to his Chinese audience, he gives them the following background information: American jazz is 350 years old, rooted in African history, and also connected to European music. He goes on to explain the significance of the African drum as a way of communicating and recording daily and cultural events.

Next, Ruff explains the power of the drum among early slaves in America. To accompany discussion, perhaps a drummer from your school's music department—or better yet, a student from the class—could give a live demonstration of the power of the drum. (You could also bring in a cassette in which the drum takes a special lead.) After hearing such "live" rhythms, most students will have to agree that it's nearly impossible to listen dispassionately to a well-played drum; the rhythms insist on full attention and engagement from the audience.

Such responses underline the point that Ruff makes when he talks about the fear white masters had about the drum's power. People move in time to rhythms; music can inspire people to act in certain ways. Just ask students for a few examples—what would a party be like without music? A church service? A funeral, wedding, or graduation?

Zinsser moves from explaining the roots of jazz to explaining how the two musicians in this piece, Ruff and Mitchell, learned jazz. Both were trained musicians whose mentors included Louis Armstrong and Duke Ellington (par. 10). They also gained teaching experience and were able to survive and thrive as artists because they could teach as well as perform (Question No. 3).

To engage students in Question No. 4, consider using the following queries to promote inductive thinking about this question: Should teachers also be accomplished practitioners in their fields?

- Should a person who works with young children *have* young children?
- Should a person who teaches science *be* a scientist?

- Should a person who teaches writing *be* a writer?
- Should a person who coaches football *be* a proficient player (or former player)?

Clearly, there are no absolutely right or wrong answers here; students should find many reasons to support both sides of this controversy.

Ruff and Tan, both masters of their art, are from different cultures, and yet they share an openness that allows them to always be learners in the field of music. For example, Ruff initially goes to Shanghai because he had already seen the tremendous connections and contributions that music from diverse cultures could offer his students at Yale. Tan, too, shares this commitment to both music and his students. Both men demonstrate their teaching prowess and their commitment to innovative pedagogy as they search the world over for ways to make music come alive for their students (Question No. 5).

In addition, Tan, Ruff, and Mitchell all struggled with certain prejudices and injustices while they were musicians. Yes, they all obtained classical educations in music, but America would not accept black musicians in classical orchestras, just as Communist China repressed art forms considered representative of Western cultures.

Certainly the Chinese educational experience differed greatly from that in the United States. How would American students feel if they had to go work the land for three months out of the year for their country? What would they learn? What would they lose?

For a ten-year period in China, students were not allowed to hear any music from the Western world. What exactly did they miss in the years between 1966 and 1976? Have students brainstorm for the popular artists and musicians in this time period. The class might work in small groups to research music under the following categories:

- Rock and Roll
- Classical
- Broadway
- Country-Western
- Instrumental

Even without research, most students will know that the Chinese missed out on the Beatles!

To dramatize the concept of improvisation, consider asking student volunteers to improvise in a number of areas. For instance, you might ask them to make a short speech based on either of the following:

- a single word or a single question based on a reading from the text
- a picture (perhaps from the photographs that introduce this thematic section)

In connection with the art of improvisation, you may want to ask students the following question: When can an artist "break the rules"? Through this discussion, you may lead students to an important concept in writing: One has to know the rules well before understanding how to break these rules effectively.

Bernice Reagon, Black Music in Our Hands (p. 306)
(Cross-Chapter Connections: "Roots and Memories," "Ways of Learning")

In contrast to William Zinsser's relatively long essay that compares the music of two national cultures (text p. 293), this piece is quite short and concentrates on one individual's musical experience within a single (yet conflicted) national culture.

To promote understanding the different roles art can play, you might want to ask students to reflect on their lives and think about their own motivations for writing imaginatively, drawing, dancing, acting, or playing an instrument. Through this reflection, they may see that, like Reagon, they use art for a variety of different reasons. For Reagon, music was initially a way for her to feel a part of a culture (par. 4–6). Later, music became a way for her to express her emotions and her beliefs (par. 7–11). Further, she discovered that through music she could affect other people (par. 12–15).

Reagon's analogy comparing music to a tool further emphasizes her point that music can be used in many ways to affect one's life and one's understanding of that life. The tool is inextricably connected to the worker; to produce anything, both are needed. Students may best grasp this analogy by viewing a pen (or a typewriter or word processor) as a tool. These writing instruments are there to serve the needs of the writer. Without the writer they can create nothing; yet without such instruments, the writer cannot connect to a community outside of him- or herself (Question No. 2).

Reagon recognizes how powerful music can be in the black community. Because she is a gifted musician, she is asked to take over as a leader during her time in jail. What the older women recognized was that if Reagon could lead people in song, she could lead them in other actions as well. In other words, she was not only a member of the chorus, but she was the director, as well (Question No. 3). In addition, Reagon must have had a great deal of courage. To prove this, ask for a volunteer from your class to lead the class in a song. Chances are, most students will not want to be the ones to have their voices heard all alone. Thus, the person who dares to sing first demonstrates at least two qualities essential for a good leader: self-confidence and courage.

Reagon defines black music in paragraphs 17–21. She says that black music is a rhythmical expression that comes from deep within a black person, an expression that both unites him or her to the community and promotes action and understanding at the same time.

After discussing Reagon's experience with music as well as their own experiences, students should be able to connect purposes for writing with purposes for singing: to express one's self, to gain insight and understanding, to be a part of a community, to entertain, to affect and inform others (Question No. 5). In this essay, Reagon seems to incorporate all of these purposes. In addition, her conclusion suggests her desire to convince people of the importance and need for music in uniting and fostering one's culture.

The Extended Thinking and Research suggestions for this essay lend themselves to oral presentations as well as research/process essays. To work with these suggestions, you may want to have students read all three essays on music in this thematic section sequentially.

Noël Bennett, Halo of the Sun (p. 311)
(Cross-Chapter Connections: "Ways of Learning," "Crossing Borders")

Striving to learn a culturally unfamiliar art form, Bennett recognizes her need for a mentor as well as for an understanding of how art relates to the history and beliefs of a culture. Students are invited to explore art and American culture, as well as ways of imparting and accumulating knowledge.

As she works to become a master weaver, Bennett discovers that, as an outsider, she is not privy to the secrets shared by the Navajo weavers. After failing to find a teacher through requests for help, Bennett decides to make her less-than-successful efforts to weave conspicuous, hoping that someone will take pity on her. Since her direct approach—as well as her observations of Navajo weavers at work—proved fruitless, the success of her new appeal suggests that she has learned something important about the culture within which she now lives (Question No. 1). She recognizes the importance of allowing them to decide to come to her rather than imposing her desire to learn on them.

Her process, then, really begins with her intense motivation to learn. She also needed the courage to recognize her own limitations and to accept the advice and criticism of an expert teacher. Under this mentor's tutelage, Bennett had to retrace her steps, so to speak, going back to spinning the wool for six months. Once her materials were ready, she began working on her actual project, collaborating with her son, Shawn, to choose a design of "a snake, a stick and the sun." After choosing the design, she concentrates on the pattern and on her technique, weaving and unraveling as she goes along. If students see a parallel between the writing process and Bennett's process, they are to be commended. And what does this process reveal about Bennett herself? Most students will see her as a persistent, dedicated, patient, talented—yet perhaps initially naive—artist (Question No. 2).

Bennett discovers that she learned because her Navajo teacher did some very wise things. First, while watching her student work, the teacher could silently assess what her strengths and weaknesses were before any formal lessons began. In other words, instead of concentrating on what she (as the expert) knew, the teacher wisely waited to see first what her student knew. Then, the teacher had her student practice over and over again. Instead of doing the work for her student, the teacher acted as a guide, watching Bennett as she did the actual work. The responsibility and deadlines, then, become solely the responsibility of the student. (As you discuss effective teaching approaches, you might ask students if they think they would work well with the mentor approach to learning and to explain why or why not.)

As they read Bennett's essay, students can compare Navajo customs as well as teaching styles. What do keeping a distance from a hogan and waiting outside, patiently, imply about Navajo values? Some students may see this behavior as ultimately respectful for the people in the hogan. The choice of visiting rests with the hosts instead of the guests.

Neighborly visits in America are often just the opposite. People come up to the door, ring a doorbell, even peer in the window to see if anyone is at home. Think about door-to-door salespeople. The person at home almost feels captive. In America, for the most part, the visitor claims more respect than the person in the home (Question No. 4).

Perhaps the hardest thing for Bennett to get used to were the long silences of the Navajo people. You can imitate this same technique by keeping silent when students ask you a question as you ponder your response for thirty seconds or so. Most of us soon become uncomfortable when faced by such quiet periods. We expect sound (words, music, and so on) to fill nearly every minute of our waking time.

This same phenomenon often occurs in another classroom sequence. Frequently, when an instructor poses a question and no one offers an immediate response, the instructor will answer his or her own question. The magical quality of Navajo silence comes to light when the courageous teacher outwaits students. Almost always before a full minute of silence has passed, someone will volunteer a response. That quiet time provides the opportunity for contemplating, and sometimes students who have not previously volunteered will be the ones to speak. Perhaps their thought patterns work differently from the instant responders, yet their ideas can add new textures and dimensions to discussion.

When Bennett discovers that Navajos considered it "bad luck to weave a snake in a rug," she stops weaving for six months. At this point, because she feels she must adhere to the Navajo beliefs for her art to be meaningful, she finds herself at a standstill. Yet her process has been so valuable she cannot undo what she has made, so now she cannot go on. However, Bennett obviously keeps this problem in the back of her mind, and she keeps learning about Navajo traditions. She is not discouraged and she is certainly not lazy. She adopts the Navajo way, whether she realizes it or not, as she waits, silently, hoping for a solution to her dilemma. Through the process of maintaining silence, she keeps learning and eventually reaches an understanding that allows respect for tradition, yet also permits her to finish her piece.

Michael Dorris, Indians in Aspic (p. 321)
(Cross-Chapter Connections: "Rights and Responsibilities," "Crossing Borders")

Since this essay deals with the popular film, *Dances with Wolves*, consider showing certain scenes on the VCR in your classroom or, as an alternative, bring in tapes of other movies or television shows that portray Native Americans.

The curious student might wonder what "aspic" is and what it has to do with Indians. Some students may have had the chance to sample aspic, but most probably have not. You may want to explain that aspic is a mold made from combining clear liquids and gelatin powder. Therefore, setting Indians in aspic is like placing them in a mold of sorts—a see-through structure that is, at best, a bit wobbly.

The first two paragraphs echo the ironically witty tone of the title. Dorris's references to white American scouting activities ("Boy Scout Order of the Arrow," "merit badges in Pawnee-bashing and animal telepathy," "white captive cum laude Campfire girl") are just a few of the phrases that reveal his attitude. Calling the main characters of the film the "With" family adds an additional example of acid humor. Why would Dorris adopt this tone? Some students may see this approach as amusing and comfortable; others may find it a bit too cynical, an approach that puts them, as readers, on the defensive.

When Dorris uses a phrase like "The Meaning of Life" and chooses to capitalize it, he is, again, writing with tongue in cheek. Here he makes a point about the producers and directors being "ultra" sensitive, and he wants to make sure the readers don't miss his point. Again, some readers may find this approach less than appealing. For one thing, readers may wonder whether Dorris is interested in writing a fair-minded critique or presenting himself as a wise know-it-all. Allow for discussion on both sides of this issue.

Although Dorris sees the film as basically an old remake of other Indian films, he does credit the film for its natural setting, attention to detail, and for using Native American actors and the language of the Lakota tribe. However, he feels *Dances with Wolves* overgeneralizes, although perhaps in different ways from other movies in this genre, and that, as a result, viewers still do not know genuine historical truths.

To promote discussion of Dorris's main point, ask students how they think he would respond if one of his friends asked him whether or not the movie was worth seeing. Dorris might respond as follows:

> Sure, go see it. It's a spectacular production, but don't expect to learn anything new about who the Native American Indians really were.

In the final sentence of his review, Dorris seems to address his readers directly, for he uses the inclusive "us" at the end. Perhaps he would like to see movie viewers become more aware of subtle messages and less taken in by the spectaculars on the big screen.

Whether or not movies and television shows should aim for truth and realism is, of course, subject to discussion. Some students may see films and television programs strictly as entertainment. Others may see the power behind such media and thus feel, as Dorris does, that directors and producers alike have a responsibility to present a balanced view. Asking students to list the five movies and television shows that have affected them the most should promote lively discussion of this issue.

Being a film critic is a harder job than it appears. You might invite students to write their own reviews, as suggested in the Extended Thinking and Research activities. As a warm-up for this assignment, consider taping one of Siskel and Ebert's weekly critiquing sessions and asking the whole class to respond to the evaluations that these two popular critics make on current movies. Encourage students to consider the criteria each critic uses to make his judgments, noting that sometimes Siskel's criteria are different from Ebert's. In addition, even when they are considering the same criteria, they often make different evaluations. Students might consider which critic they believe offers the most convincing evidence (details and examples from the films) to support his assessments. In addition, they should note that even two experts frequently disagree, demonstrating that no one "right" answer exists to questions that call for subjective judgment.

Jim Sagel, Sandra Cisneros: Sneaking Past the Guards (p. 325)
(Cross-Chapter Connections: "Roots and Memories," "Crossing
Borders")

Like Cofer in "*Casa:* A Partial Remembrance of a Puerto Rican
Childhood" (text p. 166) and Morrison in "The Site of Memory" (text
p. 223), Sagel describes a woman who has found "her literary voice in
the real voices of her people" and in her culture. If students have also
read Bill Moyers's interview with Bharati Mukherjee (text p. 79), they
may find intriguing similarities and differences among these four
women whose writing depicts or responds to different cultural
backgrounds (Puerto Rican, Black American, Mexican American,
Indian).

From reading this piece, students will be able to get in touch with
their own literary histories. Do we tend to read books only about people like us? To answer this question, you may ask students to list as
quickly as they can any books they can remember reading. How many
books/films have they seen in which a main character is black? Native
American? a woman? a man? white? Oriental? Hispanic? homosexual? heterosexual? Protestant? Jewish? Catholic? handicapped?
young? middle aged? old? By looking at their list of cultural groups,
and by considering how many are the same cultural groups to which
they belong, students should reach enlightening insights about their
own reading/viewing patterns.

Consider listing some of the categories students defined on the
board. Historically, women seldom filled traditionally heroic, active
roles in movies or books; even when women were main characters,
their roles were often passive or reactive to male characters. Few films
or books from the traditional canon have black heroes (male or
female). Why is this? Have students recall the list of "classics" they
read in high school. Under what cultural groups noted in the previous
paragraph would the main characters be listed?

Students may recognize factors that contributed to Cisneros's career
in writing. First of all, she vividly recalls the displacement of her
childhood when she and her family moved a great deal. As a shy child
she spent time alone, observing the world around her. Later, her
experience at the University of Iowa's Writer's Workshop provided a
turning point that led her to realize she could—and must—use the
voice of her own ethnic culture in her writing.

Cisneros's metaphor of being the "yellow weed" in the city cracks is particularly evocative. While other students in her Writer's Workshop were trained and grown under strict conditions ("hothouse flowers"), she had to grow wherever she could fit. No one confined her in a pot; no one told her just what to do. She found her own way ("yellow" as in bright and hopeful) in her real-life situations (Question No. 3).

Although Cisneros has discovered a voice related to the culture of her birth, like other writers, she wants to reach a broad range of readers. She also wants to be able to write for a living. Cisneros's accounts reveal how difficult it is to become a recognized writer in this country. She also reveals how hard writing is. She describes her twelve-hour days, doing the best she can just to meet deadlines and thus firmly demolishes the glamorous image some may have of a celebrated writer's life.

Cisneros's experience suggests the reality of writing for most people—even those who make a living at it. Writing doesn't come easily, and it takes a great deal of time. Most students should find comfort in knowing that even a published writer struggles and works hard to get the words right. Finding writing a difficult challenge does not indicate lack of ability; the author with a "natural talent" that allows words to flow magically and easily onto paper, forming perfect sentences of deathless prose is a mythic, idealized figure, not a flesh-and-blood writer.

Of course, students' approaches to writing will differ. Not all will find Cisneros's process workable for them. Some like to start writing as soon as they get an assignment. Others write in their heads and wait to discover a focus before they begin to put ideas on paper. Still others put off work until a deadline forces them to think and write.

Elaine Hedges, Quilts and Women's Culture (p. 331)
(Cross-Chapter Connections: "Men and Women," "Roots and Memories")

As an additional prereading/journal-writing activity, ask students to consider the cover of their textbook, which features a contemporary quilt by Chicago artist, Jane Sassaman. The quilt, which Sassaman calls "Garden Spiral," uses repeat blocks, strip piecing, and appliqué that reflect the forces she cites as her inspiration: "Black earth and the bright colors of new life." Diagonal pattern placement and the spiral forms suggest images of movement and growth. Sassaman completed this quilting project in ten weeks. Students might speculate on why this quilt was chosen for the cover—how does it reflect and reinforce the themes suggested by the book's title and by its contents?

Elaine Hedges asks readers to think not only about the history of quilting, but also to consider what this activity implies, historically, about American values, about the relationships between men and women, and about women and their communities. (The classic *Quilts in America* by Patsy and Myron Orlofsky provides a valuable supplement to this essay.)

Since Hedges contends that a patriarchal society stifles women (Spretnak's essay on "Ecofeminism" also explores this theme, text p. 228), the class discussion might center on whether women today are stifled. If so, what outlets do women pursue now that might be considered equivalent to quilting? In addition, students should also think about what creative outlets men have today.

The history of quilting can be traced to ancient times. In America, quilt making arose, as Hedges suggests, out of scarcity; because there was little cloth in early America, women made use of every scrap. However, even though quilting was a necessity, women found ways to make their products intricately beautiful and unique. Quilting bees were one social activity that fostered such creativity; regional pride also contributed to the creativity among quilters. Of course, when the Industrial Revolution came about and cloth and sewing machines were readily available, quilting was no longer a necessity.

Students are asked to draw inferences about the relationships between women at their quilting bees and men at their drinking taverns. In paragraph 5, Hedges suggests some of the relationships that existed between women. Since women at quilting bees were usually working together on one quilt, they probably sat quite close to one another; they were probably connected by the very threads with which they worked, as well as by their mutual commitment to the task. In saloons, men would usually be physically more distant.. They could stand and sit as they pleased; perhaps they played cards, but this exchange would focus on competition instead of cooperation (Question No. 3).

As students seek visual art that reflects twentieth-century America, they should discover a variety of possibilities: television commercials, magazine ads, home videos, television shows (ask for specifics here), music videos, special-effects cinematography, posters, campaign slogans, brand-name logos, and so forth.

The specific names given to quilts addressed social issues such as slavery, Christianity, state acquisitions, and the westward movement. Aspects of everyday life ("Hens and Chickens," "Duck's Foot in the Mud") as well as the longings women had ("Trip Around the World") provided titles as well. Consider asking students to think about what title they would give to a quilt planned to reflect their lives, either at home, at school, or at work.

Should we celebrate the products made by women who were basically forced into subservient positions in society? Although students may have differing opinions, most will agree that we should at least admire the creativity that arose out of such conditions.

For a unique whole-class project, consider doing the third Extended Thinking and Research suggestion. Such a project could be started midway through the semester, and the end product presented as an highly original alternative for (or part of) the final exam. The quilt might then be donated to the college. Students may also choose to research other early-American crafts or to study and analyze the quilts from their specific area of the country.

Alice Walker, Everyday Use (p. 337)
(Cross-Chapter Connections: "Ways of Learning," "Rights and Responsibilities," "Crossing Borders")

While Hedges analyzes the ties that quilting has to women in America, in this short story Walker examines how a family heirloom can bind or separate family members. Thus, students are asked to think about their own families before reading this piece, and how—and why—people grow and change, depending on their experiences.

Once they have read the story, students are asked to think carefully about the three characters they have just met. They will have little trouble characterizing the two sisters and their mother.

Maggie is the one who will always stay close to home, the homely one, the one who is good-natured. She is not "school smart," but she demonstrates the common sense and complex understanding of relationships that her highly educated sister lacks. She seems somewhat afraid of her older sister, but close and loyal to her mother.

Dee, on the other hand, is the bright and beautiful one, the one who is ambitious and determined to make a better life for herself. She has gone out into the world and sees things differently than do her mother and sister, who have remained relatively unchanged, at home. Although Dee once was ashamed of her family, she now views Maggie and her mother as quaint exhibits in her own personal museum of black history.

The *mother* tells us that she has little education, she lives with Maggie, she sings church songs, she likes to do men's work, and she is rather stout. But who is she? She probably is a woman who has struggled to raise her two girls (perhaps alone; no father is mentioned), she has worked hard, and she is relatively content with what she has achieved in life. She is also a sharp-witted observer and an insightful judge of character. Although Dee exasperates her and Maggie worries her, she loves both of her daughters. Her deep sense of fair play leads her to act out against her older daughter who, in the past, has often intimidated her mother into silence.

Maggie shares her mother's sense of humor and her understanding of human nature. Maggie and her mother may look quite plain and ordinary, but the insights they have are extraordinary. Dee, on the other hand, appears to be successful and educated, yet she can't understand the details of everyday life (Question No. 2).

Dee may have the best education, and indeed, she does know about things going on in the world that Maggie and her mother will probably always see differently (or even avoid considering). However, Maggie and her mother are educated in real-world experience; they know how to work the fields, how to milk a cow, how to be content. As a result, there is little connection between Dee and her mother and sister once she leaves the common, everyday life for a more sophisticated city existence.

Why, then, does Dee even come back home? Her clothing and her new name suggest that she has discovered the importance of getting back to her roots. In reclaiming her heritage, however, she ironically sidesteps getting significant information from her mother about her past (par. 25–31). Instead, she now wants to own old family possessions because they are culturally symbolic and financially valuable (par. 45–51; 68). Dee doesn't know or care much about the stories behind the objects; she thinks only about their impact as culturally trendy objets d'art in her city apartment (par. 52).

In contrast, Maggie and her mother value their family objects, not because they are valuable heirlooms, but because they are useful, everyday items. Maggie and her mother also know—and love—the stories and people (like Grandma Dee) behind the objects (par. 52–55).

In the end, students may recognize that both Maggie and her mother change. In the last paragraph, Maggie smiles. She is no longer scared of her sister or of being a failure in her sister's eyes. Perhaps Maggie realizes that by staying at home, she hasn't lost anything at all; she has, unlike her sister, come to know exactly who she really is. The mother has finally found the courage to stand up to Dee. No longer does she fantasize—as she does in the first scene—a wonderful moment when she will appear as her older daughter wants her to be. Instead, she accepts herself with all of her human strengths and weaknesses and declares Dee's standards extraneous to her own life.

Certainly Walker drives home the point that who we are doesn't come from books or from fancy clothes or from the fads and trends of the times. It comes from who we are in our everyday lives, what we think about in our everyday lives, and how we put our knowledge of who we are and where we came from to "everyday use."

Victor Hernandez-Cruz, urban dream (p. 345)
(Cross-Chapter Connections: "Ways of Learning," "Crossing Borders")

If students engage in the prereading exercise before reading this poem, they find it easier to see connections among the images Hernandez-Cruz creates. You may choose to have students read the poem to themselves and then write a reaction, or you may choose to give a dramatic reading while they listen. Some students may feel uncomfortable or confused by their first encounter with this assault of images; others may be disgusted. Still others will feel challenged and invigorated. Few will be either bored or completely enchanted.

Consider asking students to reread and think about the poem in small groups. One group task could be to choose appropriate music to accompany each part of the poem. Ask students to come up with specific songs that many other students would know as well. After such a discussion, have the groups meet as a whole class with a recorder from each group to describe the musical accompaniment they have planned for this poem.

The images in Part 1 are, first of all, noisy. Students should recognize the sounds as some type of tragic reaction—loud, shrill, frightening sounds. The other images—fires, bombs, walls caving in, people falling—all relate to warlike fighting.

In contrast to Part 1, the sounds in Part 2 are much more subdued: silence, whispers, crunching. The images, after the battle, are bloody and graphic; the objects that float by lifeless bodies are typical middle-class objects: steaks, furniture, leisure activities, politicians.

Once the dreams have gone by and all is destroyed, music arrives. Who will be there to dance? Does anyone survive the war? (Question No. 4).

READINGS: MEN AND WOMEN

Photographs and Previews (pp. 348–350)
Suggestions for Writing

Photographs

1. How old do you think the two people in this scene are? Explain your answer with supporting details.

    Do the people in this scene appear to have the same emotions? Explain.

2. What's the story behind this kiss?

    Why might the photographer have chosen to capture so many pedestrians in the background of this photograph?

3. A photograph, like an essay, is often united by a theme. With this thought in mind, what central theme do you see in this scene?

    If you could be present in this room, what do you imagine the man washing the clothes is saying to the woman wearing the pants?

Previews

1. Which, if any, of these quotations leads you to think that the author is writing from an objective point of view? Explain.

2. Which of these authors seems to be the most emotionally involved in the gender issue? Explain.

Cross-Reference List: Alternative Selections for "Men and Women"

Paula Gunn Allen, Where I Come from Is Like This (p. 351)
(Cross-Chapter Connections: "Ways of Learning," "Roots and Memories," "Rights and Responsibilities")

If you have a class of extremely capable and independent writers and thinkers, consider challenging them by juxtaposing this essay with "Ecofeminism" (text p. 228) and "Split at the Root" (text p. 239). All three essays deal with women's struggles to define themselves, both historically and personally. Rich's essay ("Split at the Root"), which combines narrative with analytic explanation, is perhaps the most accessible. Spretnak's "Ecofeminism," which uses extended definition to explore the topic of women's connection with nature, is the most challenging. Allen's essay, with its blend of the historical and personal and its comparisons between Native American and mainstream American life, provides a fine example of synthesis. (You could, of course, pair Rich's essay with Allen's or Spretnak's with Allen's rather than making the more complex three-way comparison.)

Before reading this selection, students are asked to think about their own roots (in the first prereading question). In addition, you may have them complete the phrases Allen uses at the end of paragraph 9:

"She told me who I was" (Who are you?), "who I was supposed to be" (Who are you supposed to be?), "whom I came from" (From whom did you come?), "and who would follow me" (Who will follow you?).

Like Rich, Allen is striving to be whole. She wants to keep her Native American heritage while being an active woman in other cultural situations. In response to Question No. 1, consider having students find the evidence in the text that points to the traditional role Allen respects (the power of femininity, par. 4; the strength and practicality, par. 5; the religious hierarchy, par. 7; the binding oral tradition, par. 8; the natural rites of passage, par. 9; the respect for one another, par. 18).

The only new characteristics Allen suggests (students will have to draw inferences to get to this point) are those that will lead Native American women to a sense of peace and oneness. She sees getting in touch with a heritage that is ancient as truly new and vital.

To respond to Question No. 2, students should think about how they would define the word *tentative*. Have them use it in a sentence and then substitute appropriate synonyms that come to mind: "unsure," "hesitant," "temporary," "indefinite" are just a few that might fit. When Allen says that none of the Indian women were tentative, she is saying then that they were sure of themselves, whole, united, defined. They knew who they were; they understood their place in the universe.

Allen further goes on to define Indian women by suggesting what they were not (Question No. 3). This question provides a fine opportunity to explain that when students attempt to write an extended definition, they can use this strategy. Students' responses regarding whether they have known people who were "foolish," "dumb," "vain" may vary. However, to pursue the danger of overgeneralizing and stereotyping, you may want to have students consider whether this person was *always* foolish, vain, and so on, or was that image just an impression based on a surface relationship?

Most students will recognize that through her historical/personal approach, Allen conveys a balance between facts and her own life experiences. You could ask students to actually count the paragraphs that are historical versus those that are personal—is the essay totally balanced? (We count ten as historical, eleven as personal.)

The stories Allen hears from her mother can be categorized under the following headings: sexuality, religion, nature, social mores, family history, emotions, actions, education, world history, social differences. In other words, her mother touched on all aspects of life and of death in her stories; the most important value for a Native American woman was to be a whole person—connected to one's soul, one's family, one's country, one's universe.

Whereas the menstrual cycle of the Native American woman is seen as a powerful yet natural part of a woman's identity, "formal, white" culture, according to Allen, thinks there is something "bad about it, that it meant you were sick, cursed, sinful, and weak . . ." (Question No. 6). This view, of course, shows women as being dependent; the Native American view, as Allen describes it, reflects a culture that respects bodily functions as normal and even empowering.

Although answers will vary as to what goals mothers wish for their children, many students may respond with traits such as "content, happy, loved" for daughters, while traits for sons may differ slightly, with the emphasis on success and fame. Of course, it's quite possible that the two lists will be almost identical as well (Question No. 7). It will be interesting to see whether the lists of men and women differ significantly as well as to note whether older students identify traits that contrast with those listed by younger students.

Before students answer or discuss Question No. 8, you may ask them to get into small groups and list/brainstorm the conflicts with which modern women must deal and, on a separate sheet, the conflicts that affect men today. You may find you have the perfect opportunity to push students to possible "causes" for these conflicts. A series of "whys" should help students get beyond an obvious cause. Example:

- Why is the woman who works outside the home still the major housekeeper in most families?

  Because there's the feeling that housework is women's work?

  Because, in many cases, the woman earns less and is, therefore, seen as contributing less?

- Why?

  Because traditionally women stayed at home and men worked.

- Why?

Allen writes that Native Americans still care for their elderly and for their orphaned children. As she writes, when Indians get old, they always know that "someone will take care" of them. The same goes for a young girl who gets pregnant. The baby and the mother are automatically taken in by the mother's family.

When students discuss whether or not these same attitudes prevail in our society, caution them against generalizing. Perhaps groups of students could research to discover how many people today are homeless, in nursing homes, in orphanages. Again, you can get students to avoid jumping on a dangerous bandwagon by asking the following question: "Just because a person is in a nursing home, can one automatically assume that the family or society doesn't care?"

Allen doesn't offer broadly based statistics to support her allegations. Some students may ask whether she based the generalization that Native American society is "less dehumanizing" solely on her own experiences and, if so, whether the generalization is then valid. Such a challenge raises serious and important issues that can lead to a lively and rewarding discussion.

Peter Filene, Between a Rock and a Soft Place: A Century of American Manhood (p. 359)
(Cross-Chapter Connections: "Roots and Memories," "Crossing Borders")

Just as Allen writes about her conflicts in harmonizing her modern life with her Native American heritage, Filene writes about the conflict that many modern American men must face. Unlike most other writers in this text, Filene avoids the use of "I" throughout this entire essay. Not only that, but he doesn't even use the editorial "we" until the last sentence in this piece.

Students should realize that when they write they have such choices available to them, and these choices make a difference, especially as far as audience and effect are concerned. There is nothing wrong with using "I" in an essay, just as there is nothing wrong with avoiding it. The intended effect justifies the approach. Consider having students choose one of their journal entries that is loaded with "I" and asking them to rewrite this entry without using the "I." Students may make two important discoveries through this short exercise: First, in almost every case, the "I" is easily erased without any loss of denotative meaning; second, the tone of a piece changes dramatically as soon as the "I" is removed.

Now you can ask the loaded question: Why might Filene have chosen to omit the "I's" from his piece while other writers, such as Rich (text p. 239), Spretnak (text p. 228), and Allen (text p. 351) use the "I" throughout when dealing with similar gender issues?

Students are asked to think about the roles and stereotypes of men and women in the prereading questions. Since Filene's essay is sure to stir interest, if not debate, allow students time to discuss these stereotypes and their notions of what it might be like to be of the opposite sex today.

Having students restate Filene's main point in one sentence (Question No. 1) asks them to write a concise summary. Students should understand that they will probably need to write many drafts of this one sentence before they can successfully synthesize the many elements in this essay. You can aid students as they work to compose an effective summarizing sentence by asking the following questions:

- What is this essay about? (The dilemma American men face today)
- So what? (This dilemma creates a conflict for men because they are torn between being strong, tough, and successful and being warmer and more supportive.)
- What are Filene's primary sources? (Historical and psychological)

Once students have identified these main parts of the essay, they may be able to construct a valid thesis that incorporates all of these parts. When students recognize Filene's main point, they can begin analyzing his sources. Are these sources valid? convincing? Having students list sources and then comment on the type of source begins the processes of analysis and evaluation. Filene uses a variety of sources, including polls, popular magazines, journals, books, and even his own lectures. You may also ask students to list which sources they believe to be most reliable.

The second question in this analysis is more crucial to examining his thesis: Does he discuss a representative population of men? In the footnote to this essay, Filene lists the occupations of those he quotes:

Hall = psychologist; Debs = union activist; Wilson = politician, president; Roosevelt = politician, president; Steffens = journalist. Four out of the five are known for their liberal attitudes; Steffens was also tagged as a radical thinker. In addition, four out of the five fathers of these men attained upper-middle-class status in this country. One final note: all five of the men are white. Filene claims this group is diverse because they come from different time periods. What do students think about his claim?

Most students should have no trouble isolating Filene's three causes (each cause is highlighted in the essay). To reinforce the idea of independent summarizing, however, ask students to construct one sentence for each cause that addresses the more important "So what" as well as the "What" in each case:

- In Victorian times, men were expected to be stoic and ambitious, a contrast to men of today, who believe in cooperation as well as competition.
- One hundred years ago, men received recognition for their heroic, manly deeds, whereas today men lack the desire and opportunity for such applause.
- When women's roles within marriage began changing, men's roles became less defined, thus creating the conflict they face today.

A point-by-point comparison will help students identify the differences and similarities Filene believes exist between fathers of today and yesterday. You may ask students to list points before beginning this exercise. Among other things, they should recognize the importance of addressing the following:

	Fathers Then	Fathers Now
Values/Beliefs		
Discipline		
Goals		
Emotions		
Behavior		
Relationships		

If the two groups appear to be more similar than different, then students should ask whether Filene's main point is justified.

Similarly, when students compare husband/wife relationships now and in the past, they should also set up a list of points to determine in a fair manner whether Filene's contention is true: Have male/female relationships changed over the course of one hundred years and, if so, to what extent?

Does Filene have goals for today's men (Question No. 7)? As he puts it, "What is the way out of this trap?" (par. 49). In his concluding paragraphs, Filene does urge men to discover for themselves the lives and values they want to have. In other words, instead of finding themselves without a strong identity, they should look to all the choices they now have and discover who they want to be. They should avoid trying to fit either stereotype—the macho man or the mild-mannered reporter—and act in the way they see fit.

The logical follow-up question, "How do men do that?" is really not addressed. Filene certainly doesn't expand on any social or political steps men, as a group, might take. (For example, he makes no proposal that would equate with the women's movement that began in the late 1960s and continues today.) Does this lack of specific suggestions weaken the essay? Can students themselves suggest means of action? Do students think men should form groups, petition, or lobby in order to make their lives better? Play the devil's advocate on this one, asking students to question whether or not men really do face the conflict Filene describes.

The Extended Thinking suggestions allow students to model Filene's historical approach either by addressing the place of women in the last one hundred years or by considering any gender role from another culture's point of view. To be effective (and fair), students who choose this writing task should seek a variety of sources; this challenging research project requires a great deal of time and would work well as a semester-long activity.

Alexis de Tocqueville, How Americans Understand the Equality of the Sexes (p. 376)
(Cross-Chapter Connections: "Rights and Responsibilities," "Crossing Borders)

In this essay, de Tocqueville gives readers a different perspective from those of the three previous essays. First of all, he reflects on American society as he observed it a hundred and fifty years ago. Second, he comments as an outsider, a visitor from another country and culture. In the prereading questions, students are asked to think about how men and women view each other today. However, as they read the essay, they should keep this question in the back of their minds: Assuming that de Tocqueville's observations are valid, do his comments apply to men and women of today?

Some students may find the style and language of this piece a bit more difficult to understand than those of contemporary writers. Therefore, encourage them to take their time with this piece and to annotate with particular care any sections that remain puzzling after an initial reading.

Even though they may have some difficulty with the vocabulary, students should recognize that Tocqueville held American women in high esteem. Some, however, may express concern that to praise the strength and energy of American women he found it necessary to equate them with men. In paragraph 4, for instance, he describes the typical American woman: She "exhibits a masculine strength of understanding and a manly energy" yet has the "great delicacy of personal appearance and always retains the manners of women." Woman's role is to take an equal part in the association of marriage with her husband and to fulfill the tasks that need to be done by her.

In contrast, de Tocqueville believes that women in Europe are not really considered equal to their male counterparts. European women, according to the author, are "considered as seductive but imperfect beings" (par. 8). Man may compliment them as they act timid and demure, but in Europe women are used by men, whereas in America women are guided by men (par. 8, 9). This, perhaps, is the greatest distinction of all. Consider asking students to write, in their own language, what de Tocqueville implies in these paragraphs. Certainly, they should notice that in spite of his admiration for American women, de Tocqueville still sees them as justifiably subject to the "guidance" of men.

When students get to Question No. 3 regarding de Tocqueville's views on sexual indiscretions and rape, expect arguments to follow, especially in light of modern-day rape trials and punishments for female prostitutes as compared to their male patrons. Actually, to hold a fair discussion here, you might consider asking different groups to research the number of rapes that go to trial and the results, the number of reported rapes each year, the number of repeat offenders, and the statistics and laws concerning prostitution in your specific state.

Also, expect controversy as to whether or not one should perform a role primarily for the good of one's country. You may want to list the following topics on the board and ask students to put them in order according to what Americans value most: God/Higher Being, Country, Community, Family, Individual. Most students will admit that this list works exactly in reverse for most modern Americans; therefore, performing a role for one's country—whether it be going to war or remaining behind to "keep the home fires burning"—will not satisfy the majority of today's students.

Question No. 5 leads students to see that de Tocqueville compares women's position in America to women's positions elsewhere in the world, probably Europe. The "loftier position," to him, is that role in which a woman can be dependent, yet strong; obedient, yet intelligent; equal, yet different. (You may find that, given the first two pairs of adjectives in this list, students question strongly his definition of both "equal" and "different.")

To de Tocqueville, the American system of democracy allows both men and women to assume different roles while remaining equal in one another's eyes. The strength of democracy, according to the author, is in its system that accepts and encourages differences, and at the same time promotes equality. The potential drawback, however, is that one group (women, in particular) cannot escape from its assigned role. As de Tocqueville observed in the nineteenth century, women in America willingly accepted the role, or "yoke," they were assigned—at least the most "virtuous" did! (Some historical research might be in order to discover women who did not accept this yoke—could any of them be called "virtuous"? You might also ask whether de Tocqueville speaks only of white women or whether his generalizations seem intended for black and Native American women as well.)

Students who would like to know more about de Tocqueville's philosophy are directed to two primary sources in the Extended Thinking suggestions. Some students may be moved to challenge de Tocqueville's observations and to converse in writing with the author about his view of male and female roles (Suggestion No. 2).

Brent Staples, Just Walk on By: A Black Man Ponders His Power to Alter Public Space (p. 381)
(Cross-Chapter Connections: "Arriving," "Ways of Learning," "Crossing Borders")

In contrast to Filene's historic approach, Staples chooses to use his personal experience to explain his point: Because he is a black male, women are afraid of him. The prereading questions ask students to think about how they might appear to others and how, at times, we all make judgments based on initial appearances. If your teaching style includes informal humor, you can prove how much we react to people's appearances by altering your own appearance on this par-ticular class day. Wear something out of the ordinary or comb your hair in a different fashion. If the change is dramatic enough, students will certainly respond in some way to your altered appearance.

If students have done the third prereading exercise, they will be more likely to connect their initial thoughts with the first discussion question following the reading of this essay. Depending on their reactions, students will be able to judge more objectively whether the woman's reaction was a common one.

Whether or not the reaction is justified should elicit some discussion. Have students point to the facts: It's late, the street is deserted, the woman is young and alone, the man is young, tall, and casually dressed.

Students need to think objectively here. If everything else were the same, except it was daytime, would she be as scared? If the black man were wearing a suit, would she be as scared? If the man were white, tall, young, and casually dressed? In other words, Staples's point is that she is scared because he is a black man—does this example support his point? (If students agree that the woman is most scared because he is black, then the incident supports the author's point.)

In this essay, Staples is most likely so surprised at the young woman's terrified reaction because, as he states in paragraph 7, he is from a small town in Pennsylvania. In this town, he was, as he puts it, "one of the good boys"—the shy kid who never bought into the macho lifestyle of so many of the others in his neighborhood. When the woman runs from him, he realizes that in a big city, in a strange city, many people react to others based on prior fears.

Staples is "surprised, embarrassed, and dismayed" at this first incident, and, although he doesn't state this outright, he also seems saddened and disillusioned by this reaction. He could have also felt anger or hatred, but neither one of these emotions is apparent in this piece. In retrospect, he remains gentle and introspective.

Where does the concept of "black as dangerous" come from? You may ask students to keep an exact list of all the crimes, both national and local, that they find in the local newspaper. Who are the most likely perpetrators of crime, according to this list? White men? Black men? White-collar workers? Blue-collar workers? White women? Black women? Consider having groups make lists and then hold a whole-group discussion on what each group has found.

In addition to this survey, consider how deeply a person's experiences affect his or her outlook. How deeply might one incident affect a person's outlook?

Most students should have little trouble following Staples's main point. Although the incidents of prejudice have enraged him in the past, he seeks in this piece to open people's eyes to how quick we are to judge a person, based more on the fear of race than on the facts or our prior experiences.

In the end, what Staples has discovered is how important appearance and demeanor are in the company of strangers. Staples's solution—that of whistling classical songs while he walks late at night—reveals that he is not only a realist, but also a creative person, with a wry, self-sustaining sense of humor. Since people judge surface impressions, then he will add to his demeanor a calm, intellectual note with his classical music. Is it too much to hope that, through this quietly creative act, he may even alter some people's stereotyped views that all black men are dangerous and ought to be feared? Staples's analogy of the cowbell reflects on the position a black man often finds himself in within the United States: One is safe in this hunting atmosphere only when one makes harmonious sounds instead of growling. For fear alone can cause a frightened hunter to pull the trigger without really looking carefully at the prey.

Students can increase their awareness of media stereotyping by watching a variety of television shows that include black male characters. Again, this activity lends itself to group collaboration. The more shows members within the group view, the stronger inferences the group can draw.

Alice Walker, The Right to Life: What Can the White Man Say to the Black Woman? (p. 386)
(Cross-Chapter Connections: "Roots and Memories," "American Dreams and Creations," "Rights and Responsibilities")

Before students read Walker's prose poem, you may want to assign any of the following selections to provide background information on the black experience in the United States: "Slave Ship" (text p. 42), "I Remember Papa" (text p. 106), "Learning to Read and Write" (text p. 151), "Finishing School" (text p. 171), "Shanghai Blues" (text p. 293), "Black Music in Our Hands" (text p. 306), "Everyday Use" (text p. 337). Some of this prior knowledge will aid students in understanding the references Walker makes in this piece.

In addition to this, students can prepare to read Walker's scathing indictment by writing about situations in which they felt controlled, exploited, or treated unjustly. They may, of course, write about an event they witnessed instead of a direct experience.

The selections in the next section of the text focus on persuasion, and this piece serves as a useful bridge to demonstrate writing that pursues more than one aim. Certainly Walker explains, but, in addition, she writes and speaks to move her audience. As students read this selection and as they read the selections in Section Four, they should pay special attention to the importance of connotation. Thus, for Question No. 1 encourage them to pick out not only images that move them, but also single "loaded" words. ("Womb"—instead of "body" or "selves"—is such an example in the third line.) They should be able to conclude that the more specific Walker gets ("twenty generations," "twenty-one children," "Saturday nights"), the more powerful her language becomes.

The graphic details and the facts Walker provides almost certainly evoked profound empathy and agreement from most of her original audience—participants in a pro-choice rally. Certainly, few could hear this speech and go away unmoved.

Students may be surprised at several incidents to which Walker refers—babies were murdered, children were taken from mothers, women were forced to be sterilized, 30 million African children died on the way to the Americas, and so on. If students question any of Walker's claims, encourage them to find another source on the subject to seek corroboration or opposing claims.

Certainly, Walker organized this piece to appeal directly to a live audience. In a sense, she was giving a performance, and thus she had the responsibility of keeping her audience on her every word. The repeated words and phrases serve much the same purpose as the refrain of a poem or a song. These lines serve to unite listeners and to focus their attention on the central message. By the end of this speech, the refrain almost surely remained alive in the hearts of all who heard Walker speak. (As you discuss the nature of this speech, consider relating good writing to a good performance to help students understand the responsibility writers have to their audience. The performance metaphor further incorporates the stages of revision, collaboration, and publication.)

To brainstorm several choices for Question No. 5, you may ask students to reflect on the essays they have read thus far in the semester. What groups have the "white men" Walker addresses controlled to a certain extent? (Black men, immigrants, Jews, Asians, Native Americans, women, the poor.) "Black women," then, holds not only the denotation of this specific group but may also in some ways serve as an image representing any group—not necessarily black and not necessarily female—that has been denied its basic rights, freedoms, and respect.

When students get to Question No. 6, you may ask them to think about whether an absolute statement can be considered true. Does Walker intend readers/listeners to take this line as true? More than likely, she is after an effect—she wants to incite some reaction from the audience. When she teams the word "children" with a phrase like "absolute hatred," she has, symbolically, set up a situation of innocence versus evil. And this universal struggle, this pull of right against wrong, is an ethical appeal whose roots can be traced back to Socrates.

Endings, in performances as well as in writing, are crucial, for this is the last chance a writer/actor has to move the audience. Students may grasp the beauty of endings if you ask them the following question about their own drafts: If you could leave the reader with only one thought, what would it be?

That's exactly what Walker does in this speech. She leaves the audience waiting for, thinking about, an answer. She has, in essence, pulled the audience to this conclusion. Writers who can create powerful endings will almost certainly gain—and keep—the attention of their readers.

For additional current, controversial texts written by women for women, refer students to *Revolution from Within*, by Gloria Steinem, or Susan Faludi's *Backlash: The Undeclared War Against Women*. Suggestions for Extended Thinking and Research also encourage students to delve further into specific injustices in American history or to give their own speech on a controversial issue.

Joanna Russ, When It Changed (p. 391)
(Cross-Chapter Connections: "Rights and Responsibilities," "American Dreams and Creations," "Crossing Borders")

Although this piece is clearly fictional, students should wonder in what ways it is relevant to their own life situations. Before reading this short story, students may project their own views of a sexually homogeneous world. This prewriting exercise lends itself to small- and whole-group discussions that take the form of structured debates (a free-for-all on this subject may degenerate into a shouting match). In addition to identifying which group might have the easier time, make sure students justify their responses by asking them why they think this way.

After reading Russ's story, students may suggest several possible meanings for the "It" of the title. "It" can be the world of women; "It" can also be what happened when the world of men and women ended; in addition, "It" can refer to the relationship between Katy and Janet.

What is this relationship like? In many ways, Katy and Janet assume the roles often attributed to husbands and wives today. For example, Katy, "drives like a maniac," is capable of fixing things around the house, is more emotional, and is afraid of guns. Janet, on the other hand, does most of the talking when they meet the men, and of the two women, she is the taller. However—unlike many husbands and wives today— they seem to treat each other as equals, assuming mutual responsibility for the children and their home.

The women's reactions vary when they see the four men on their planet. Katy seems anxious, almost excited, perhaps scared, she is described as looking "very pale" when she is with the men. Janet is shocked, almost disgusted, but she remains polite. Lydia was "embarrassed," and Yuki, the daughter, is curious and honest. Except for Yuki, all the other women seem to stand back and let the men speak first. Is this typical? Most students will see the reactions— intimidated, polite, embarrassed, disgusted—as all too common responses. None of the women in this story seems comfortable with the presence of men. Are most women today comfortable with men who are strangers?

The main man in the party that arrives at Whileaway reacts to the women in a respectful but firm manner. He listens, but then he gives his opinion. He tells them what he thinks and why he thinks it, and then he goes on to try to convince them to his way of thinking. He plays his role in the way he thinks will work best. He doesn't want to upset the women because he is intent on setting up a relationship so that he and other men can join them on Whileaway.

Do the women need men on Whileaway? The men in the story think so, but what about Russ—can we tell what the author thinks? As Janet explains life on her planet, it seems that this population of women lacks little. They have good soil and climate, a steady government, and a gene pool that produces highly intelligent people. This fictional world seems quite sufficient, quite independent. The women do not seem to be missing anything else at all.

When the man says he can't tell who plays the man in Katy and Janet's marriage, he is actually saying he can't tell which one dominates, or controls, the other. His statement suggests his discomfort with relationships that cannot be neatly categorized in terms of power. In addition, this comment suggests his preoccupation with sex roles and with sexuality. Rather than envisioning the fullness of Katy and Janet's relationship, he focuses on what might or might not happen in their bedroom.

As an alternative to the first Extended Thinking and Research suggestion, consider asking groups of students to compile lists of books, movies, and television shows in which women are the heroes. Initially, students may find they have a hard time coming up with lists—certainly, man as hero has dominated American culture, for the most part, but students will almost certainly name *Thelma and Louise* and *Fried Green Tomatoes* as films that feature strong and interesting women.

Many students enjoy the challenge of writing a bit of fiction themselves. Students are often most willing to share such writing. In addition, you may offer an imaginative assignment as a group venture or as an option for a series of journal entries. Besides writing an ending or another version of the story, students might write their own one-act play and perform it for the rest of the class.

Audre Lorde, The Women of Dan Dance with Swords in Their Hands to Mark the Time When They Were Warriors (p. 399)
(Cross-Chapter Connections: "Arriving," "Crossing Borders")

Although the prereading question does ask students to think about their image of "warriors" (an image that most students will identify as violent and male), it may also be beneficial to discuss the women's suffrage movement of the late nineteenth and early twentieth centuries and the more recent women's movement that began in the 1960s. Students should think about what leads groups of people to rebel. Can those who protest social injustice with marches, with petitions, with hunger strikes, with sit-ins be termed warriors?

Before students read this poem, you may want to ask them to consider the title—does the action of dancing with swords conform to a typical warrior image? Once they have discussed their varying images of warriors, they may be more apt to see the subtle comparisons implied in this poem.

In the first five lines, for example, Lorde refers to mythical and biblical stories in which a single deity or a group of gods rule the earth (Question No. 1). In contrast to the powerful life-and-death source described in the first lines, woman comes as a strong, yet vulnerable warrior who is aware of the sacrifices she must make.

The darkness in this poem may suggest the goddess as a being of color who directly contrasts to the all-white image of the gods. The darkness also sets a serious, mystical mood—perhaps night is when the goddess is most powerful.

Most students will have no trouble recognizing the conflict between men and women in this poem. Lorde cuts through the traditional image of the all-white, male higher being. A female force, with her laughter, her warmth, her wise words, her nurturing body may be more capable of controlling the world than would be her male counterpart.

If students read this poem aloud, they will "hear" the narrator's voice, strong and sure. The choice of first person indicates self-awareness and confidence while the lack of contractions gives a slightly formal, official tone. Perhaps the word that best characterizes the speaker in this poem is "powerful"—no word or phrase suggests that the speaker is the slightest bit hesitant.

SECTION FOUR
WRITING TO PERSUADE

READINGS: RIGHTS AND RESPONSIBILITIES
Photographs and Previews (pp. 418–420)
Suggestions for Writing

Photographs

1. What generalizations could you make about the people demonstrating in this scene?

Why do the people holding the sign look happy instead of, say, angry or sad?

2. Compare the expressions of this group of demonstrators with those in the photograph above. How do you explain the differences of emotion?

How would you characterize this group of demonstrators?

3. What, besides the poster sentiments, separates or distinguishes these two groups of people?

Why might the photographer have intended to have the flag on one side of this picture and the court house on the other?

Previews

1. Of all these issues—women's rights, abortions, discrimination, prejudice, the right to bear arms—which do you think is most significant today?

2. Choose one statement from these quotations and explain why you disagree with it.

Cross-Reference List:
Alternative Selections for "Rights and Responsibilities"

Selection	Text Page
Slave Ship	42
From Steerage to Sweatshop	45
Arrival at Manzanar	63
Crossing the Border	70
I Remember Papa	106
Learning to Read and Write	151
Ecofeminism: Our Roots and the Flowering	228
How the Americans Understand the Equality of the Sexes	376
The Right to Life: What Can the White Man Say to the Black Woman?	386
Should Hiroshima Have Been Bombed?	587
Hiroshima: An Act of Terrorism	596

Elizabeth Cady Stanton, The Solitude of Self (p. 421)
(Cross-Chapter Connections: "American Dreams and Creations," "Men and Women")

Before students delve into Stanton's ideology, which argues for the goals and aspirations she proposes for American women, they are asked to connect their own thinking to her three basic topics: feminism, the meaning of life, and the importance of solitude.

The first discussion question asks students to draw a first impression of the speaker. As they project their impressions, encourage them to imagine details. Is she a stern-looking woman? Is she tiny and frail? Is she tall and bold? Whatever visual picture students draw should, in some way, relate to her speaking style: Her words are simple and direct, yet her message is strong. Of course this question also raises the issue of whether or not physical appearances—including facial expressions and body language—usually reflect (or affect) a speaker's style or whether that style exists solely in the writer's choice of words, use of figurative language, and selection of rhetorical strategies.

Having students find the basic platform in this piece will help them to recognize and to write strong arguments. As Stanton writes (par. 4), "The strongest reason for giving women all the opportunities . . . is the solitude of personal responsibility of her own individual life." In other words, each person on this earth, whether male or female, must be accountable for his or her own decisions, his or her own life. Stanton describes this concept of individuality as "our own Protestant idea" (line 3). (If you are teaching in a setting that allows exploration of religious issues, you may want to ask students why Stanton would describe "the solitude of personal responsibility" as a "Protestant" ethic and whether they agree with her observation.)

Stanton begins this piece with an appeal to logic as she sets up her points with the transitions *secondly, thirdly, fourthly,* and so on. However, her argument soon takes on an emotional tone when she writes, "We come into this world alone . . . we leave it alone" (par. 6). An appeal to the audience's sense of decency immediately follows this paragraph when she states, "Again, we ask for the complete development *for the general good*" (par. 8). And it is on this sense of righteousness that her argument continues and is, for the most part, based.

Interspersed throughout her general ethical appeal are tiny "emotional catches." Have students look for the loaded language here —phrases like "broken friendship," "shadows of our afflictions," "darkest tragedies," "divine heights," and so on.

Students may initially state that yes, the author is a devout believer in God and America. If so, ask them to point to any phrases that uphold this view. They will find no direct allusions to God or America. Nor will they find instances where Stanton has quoted from the Bible (a common practice among many arguers) or from the Constitution. Instead, she creates analogies that carry her beliefs forward—analogies of sailors and soldiers going through life alone. These analogies (Question No. 6) serve to show the commonalities that women have with men. Further, these analogies reinforce the view of woman as strong and courageous and, in addition, suggest her position as a protector and defender.

Students may protest that Stanton does, indeed, mention the human soul throughout this piece, but you might point out that she does not mention it in relation to a hierarchy or a religion, per se. (You may ask students to list traditional biblical views of women; many of these images suggest why Stanton avoids such reference.)

According to Stanton, the benefits to assuming responsibility for one's own life are many. Thought becomes deeper, actions become more meaningful, philosophies are developed. From this point, the family, too, benefits. An independent woman will encourage independence and a sense of responsibility in her children; she will support her husband in his need for solitude. In addition, she will be diplomatic in the community, and she will uphold and respect the individual nature of others. From this basis, the family, community, and country become stronger and more moral.

Students will describe Stanton's philosophy of life differently; however, the concepts she espouses might include the following:

> individual/self
>
> opportunities/freedom
>
> happiness/development
>
> aloneness/solitude

It may be interesting for students to compare their responses to the second prereading question, "For me, life is like . . .," with Stanton's philosophy.

Judith Jarvis Thomson, A Defense of Abortion (p. 427)
(Cross-Chapter Connections: "Men and Women," "American Dreams and Creations")

Although most students have strong views on abortion, many have not taken the time to look at the complexities of taking a "pro-life" or "pro-choice" stance. This retrospective view written before *Roe v. Wade* and favoring the legalization of abortion provides a historical dimension that defines many of the issues related to the question of abortion. Some students may find this piece rather difficult. Thomson looks at her topic with painstaking thoroughness like a scientist peering for hours into a microscope. However, the vocabulary in this piece is quite accessible, and the analogies enable most students to understand the connections that Thomson makes.

In 1971, the abortion question was as fiercely debated as it is today. Keeping in mind the emotions aroused by this subject, Thomson recognizes the importance of conveying a fair-minded ethos. She takes logical, thoughtful steps in her argument, and, in addition, she constantly anticipates and demonstrates keen understanding of the counterargument. Unlike many pieces—pro-choice or pro-life—that students may have read, this essay focuses primarily on rational arguments rather than emotional or ethical appeals.

To explain her chain of reasoning, Thomson uses several extended analogies. The central comparison, that of the violin player, is the most significant. In this analogy, Thomson focuses on a powerful and difficult question: Are we obligated by law to sustain another person's life, to share our life with that person, no matter what our individual circumstances?

Some students may view the house metaphor as equally significant since the mother is seen as an entity unto herself, a place invaded rather than a person with free will. Like the violinist analogy, the metaphor of the house appears several times in the essay. The analogy of the brothers and the box of candy (par. 23) illustrates the problem of whether we are morally obligated to share what we have with others. Like the other analogies in this essay, the brothers with the box of candy provides images to which most people can relate. Such comparisons make the claims in Thomson's argument easier to understand than they might be if left in the abstract.

Throughout most of this essay, Thomson takes a careful, logical approach to her topic. As she draws near the conclusion of her argument, she brings in the story of the Good Samaritan. Some students may find this uncharacteristic, actually out of place for this piece. However, you might ask students what Thomson hopes to gain by using this biblical story. Perhaps she seeks to indicate that she is familiar with the Bible and with religious ethics, anticipating counterarguments that might characterize her as disdainful of traditional religious views.

After reading this piece, students should answer the question: Just what is Thomson advocating? Is she advocating abortion on demand? Is she advocating abortion as a convenient birth control method? Is she advocating stricter abortion laws? Some students may recognize that if Thomson had to join a group, she would be the perfect leader for those who espouse situation ethics. Such a group would advocate the most ethical and moral choice, based on the individual's situation (par. 47).

Throughout this piece, Thomson distinguishes between three terms: *illegal, indecent,* and *immoral.* Students should have little trouble defining the first word in terms of a person's individual rights. The next two terms are quite close in meaning and involve more than the individual. *Immoral,* however, focuses on that which is unjust and unfair. *Indecent* (par. 33, 34) also suggests wrongdoing, but the action is not necessarily unjust (as Thomson says, a person can be "callous, greedy, stingy—but not unjust") (par. 35). Students may or may not agree on Thomson's definition for these last two terms. To many students, *indecent* may be synonymous with *immoral.*

If students have read Elizabeth Cady Stanton's essay (text p. 421), they should certainly be able to compare these two authors. If Stanton were alive today, would she agree with Thomson? Many students may see several similarities between these two authors, despite the fact that they are speaking in different centuries about the rights of American women.

Greg Keath, Abortion Is Not a Civil Right (p. 443)
(Cross-Chapter Connections: "Men and Women," "Crossing Borders")

Unlike Thomson (text p. 427), who delves into the many reasons why she believes abortion should be legal, Keath focuses on why black women have such a high incidence of abortions. Before reading this short piece, students should think independently about which groups of people might have more abortions. They should also discuss in what ways poverty might affect a woman's choice to have an abortion.

Although Keath stays away from direct accusations, after students have read this piece, most will see that he believes the rise of abortions among black women results from the prejudice of whites who hold positions of authority. Keath believes that the real victim of abortion is the black race, a group he sees as targeted by Planned Parenthood clinics in inner-city areas. He urges black women to "resist the forces that drive black women to seek abortions."

Keath believes that black women are often pressured into having an abortion. You may want to ask students what evidence he offers for this position (one teenager's experience, par. 3). In this same paragraph, he says black women are also discouraged from carrying a fetus to term because motherhood is a "threat to educational hopes or aspirations to economic independence." Students may brainstorm for other possible causes as well. In addition to thinking of other causes, students should question whether or not these same pressures are present for women of other races who have unwanted pregnancies.

Keath's position does not agree with the position of many black leaders (par. 5). For example, in contrast to Jesse Jackson, Keath sees abortion as a segregation issue, not a civil-rights issue. To support this belief, Keath refers to Sanger's writings in her first book, *Pivot of Civilization*. From this piece, he chooses two direct quotations that denounce the Negro race. Again, you want students to raise the question: Do these two quotations supply adequate evidence to depict Sanger as a "Hitlerite"? Might these quotations, in context, carry a connotation different from Keath's implications?

By using Sanger as his target, Keath creates a parallel between what happened to the "undesirable races" under Hitler and the recent condition of blacks in relation to the abortion issue. There is no question that Keath sees abortion trends as a potential means—an intended means—of sterilization. He raises an emotionally charged issue, but through his historical, instead of contemporary, references, he distances himself as a speaker, perhaps to suggest the ethos of a fair-minded, impartial, and scholarly writer.

If students read and discuss this piece carefully, and if they see what position Keath holds (he is the founder of Black Alliance for Family), they will surely see that Keath would like blacks to become more independent, more responsible in their decisions concerning unwanted pregnancies. An implied agenda is that he would like to see black women choosing against abortion not for themselves or for their babies, but as a way to guard against what he believes is the white conspiracy to do away with the black race.

If students have read either Stanton's essay (text p. 421) or Thomson's essay (text p. 427), the last discussion question is particularly challenging. While these three writers may seem to agree on thoughtful and responsible independence for women, Keath's audience seems to be primarily black women, Stanton's audience upper- or middle-class white women, and Thomson's audience women of all races, from all social classes. You might ask students whether they see any of these speakers as having hidden agendas that relate to their own concerns rather than primarily to the concerns of the women about whom they write.

Students are urged to find out more about Margaret Sanger through independent research. Those who want to know more about Sanger's life can be directed to a recent biography called *Women of Valor: Margaret Sanger and the Birth Control Movement in America,* by Ellen Chester.

William Bradford Reynolds, Equal Opportunity, Not Equal Results (p. 446)
(Cross-Chapter Connections: "American Dreams and Creations," "Crossing Borders")

Because many students may be unfamiliar with issues related to affirmative action legislation in America, have them complete at least one of the prereading questions so that they can see the causes and effects of inequalities in the working world. At the very least, a discussion of the first topic should show that this issue is one that can be hotly debated in many different ways.

To connect students to this reading, you may ask them to list three of Reynolds's statements with which they agree or disagree. A discussion might follow, or such lists may serve as springboards for an extended writing assignment.

In paragraph 2, students will be able to find a possible response to Question No. 1. Reynolds establishes a rational, logical ethos in this piece. His whole argument is based on his definition of affirmative action, which he sees as a "measure for ensuring opportunity," but not necessarily for guaranteeing "results."

Reynolds goes on to claim that employers cannot promise equal results for several reasons. First of all, although all people may get a chance to come in the door, talents and abilities vary (par. 3). Secondly, an employee with seniority shouldn't be asked to give up a position to provide opportunity to a member of an underrepresented group (par. 16). You may ask students if employers could use either one of these reasons to hide any discriminatory practices.

As a polished rhetorician, Reynolds openly airs the opponents' complaints. As he writes, "The criticism, of course, is that we do not go far enough" (par. 7). To counterargue this point, Reynolds cites the landmark Supreme Court case of the *Firefighters Local Union No.*

1784 v. Stotts, noting the unfairness of disregarding seniority systems in hiring and firing decisions. In addition to this, he argues that people should be hired based on their talents and abilities, not on the color of their skin.

Reynolds interprets Title VII as basically urging that an employer consider the individual job applicant, not the group to which the individual belongs. Students should wonder what the author's purpose is in writing this piece. Were any conflicts in hiring practices (usually involving women or blacks) in the news in 1986? Why might Reynolds feel the need to address affirmative action? (A trip to the *New York Times Index, 1986* may provide some answers here.)

Reynolds's basic argument comes down to this: Affirmative action should ensure only that whoever comes through the door gets a chance to be heard. However, if students haven't already raised the question, you might: Is the road to this door the same for everyone in this country? Do all people, from all backgrounds, receive equal educations? (A flashback to the selections included in "Ways of Learning" [text pages 148–202] should give students details and examples to address for this question.) Even if students have little interest in Reynolds's legal argument, on a personal level they should be able to decide whether equal opportunity in this country is a fact or a myth. In addition, whether or not they agree with Reynolds, they should see that accepting the logic of his argument requires accepting his definition of affirmative action. Those who disagree with Reynolds may want to write their own definition.

Jesse Jackson, Why Blacks Need Affirmative Action (p. 453)
(Cross-Chapter Connections: "American Dreams and Creations," "Crossing Borders")

Since Jackson's view opposes Reynolds's (text p. 446), arguing that affirmative action needs to do more for black Americans, this piece should be read in conjunction with Reynolds's argument. However, and perhaps prior to reading either piece, students should be given the opportunity to explore their own reactions and feelings when dealing with discrimination or preferential treatment. Regardless of race or color, most of us have felt "prejudged," whether based on our appearance or an untrue rumor. And almost all students who grew up with siblings can find one instance to write about when they think someone else was awarded preferential treatment over them.

Reynolds believes affirmative action, as he defines it, provides a legal and practical means to ensure equal opportunity for employment to all people. Jackson clearly disagrees. He cites evidence to support his view that in spite of affirmative action legislation—and in spite of the claims of some whites that affirmative action unfairly favors minorities—blacks are still victims of discrimination in the job market. Jackson believes that "reverse discrimination" is an illogical term, because it implies that the white majority has passed laws to discriminate against itself. To the contrary, Jackson argues, the white majority has simply affirmed legislation that gives up an unfair advantage.

Throughout this piece, Jackson lists statistics to show the un-balanced ratio of whites to blacks in professional positions. Students should think in term of causes here: What reasons can they offer to explain why so few blacks become doctors or lawyers?

Students should also take their time and dwell on the statistics that Jackson presents in paragraph 5. Is he being fair? What is he failing to present? He gives the percentage of increase for white students in law school, but he fails to give the increase for minorities. You may ask students to do the math that Jackson has omitted.

In contrast to Reynolds's matter-of-fact/authoritative tone, Jackson's appeal holds a sense of urgency, perhaps in response to the *Bakke v. University of California* lawsuit in which Bakke, who is white, argued that that he had been denied admission because of affirmative action quotas. Since Bakke won this case, Jackson may have felt that he had an immediate responsibility to set the record straight: "In short, it is a myth that blacks are making progress at white expense" (par. 5).

As an advocate for equality and as one who feels that blacks still lag behind as far as opportunities are concerned, Jackson might very well propose that whenever possible an employer should hire a black person in order to speed up the economic opportunities for black people in general. Reynolds, of course, would be totally against this idea. As Reynolds repeats throughout his essay, he believes affirmative action should be directed toward individuals, not races or groups of people.

To gain insight on the issue of affirmative action, students might research the controversy surrounding the Bakke case. The *New York Times Index, 1978* or the *Reader's Guide to Periodical Literature, 1978* should provide sources.

Andrew Sullivan, Here Comes the Groom (p. 456)
(Cross-Chapter Connections: "Crossing Borders")

Although many students may initially disagree with Sullivan's argument that gay couples should be allowed to marry, his logical, law-based approach may convince some that this proposal isn't so far-fetched. To prepare for reading about and discussing this issue, students can writeabout and discuss their views on marriage versus living together, as well as on how they feel about gay marriages.

Because this topic will almost certainly raise strong responses, you may want to set the tone for the discussion. First of all, let your class know that everyone should be free to express an opinion without the fear of ridicule. You might also note that in any group, statistics indicate that at least 10 percent of the individuals will be homosexual. Discussion, then, should take place in an atmosphere that recognizes the sexual diversity that is part of the culturally varied classrooms in which we all study and teach.

Sullivan considers his proposal to allow gay marriages to be conservative. He argues that by engaging in a standard civil ceremony, gays will enter the mainstream of society. In a marriage, a gay couple would abide by the legalities of a contract that has long been regarded as a traditional part of the world in which we live.

In paragraphs 3–6, Sullivan explains why he believes "domestic partnership" laws are not the best solution. As he suggests, such laws do not make clear who qualifies for such a relationship. In other words, domestic partnership provisions might allow friends who live together or even seminarians to sue one another for benefits. Sullivan sees marriage as a better solution for gay couples for the following reasons: marriage provides a more stable environment (par. 6); marriage allows gays to join in the social mainstream (par. 9); marriage may encourage gays to be more responsible in their relationships (par. 10); gays would receive legal as well as social benefits (par. 11); and finally, gay marriages would provide models of commitment for other gays (par. 14).

Once students have grasped the basic reasons that Sullivan offers, they should be prepared to state their own reactions to his thoughts. They may also raise objections that Sullivan has failed to include (like the effect of such marriages upon the children either partner may have from previous heterosexual relationships). In addition, students should think about the validity of each reason the author offers. Does marriage make one more responsible? To answer this, students can look to their own family experiences. Finally, students may want to consider whether Sullivan's proposal serves to enforce negative stereotypes about gay relationships.

In the end, students should also pause to consider Sullivan's last question. This final statement includes several "loaded" words: "unfaithful, undeveloped, and insecure." Students should wonder what factor, or combination of factors, makes a relationship work. Is it the legal contract? Is it something else? Is it a combination of legal and personal issues that contribute to secure and faithful relationships?

Depending on the interest and openness with which the class has responded on this issue, you may consider inviting gay rights advocates into the class to speak with your students. In addition, students are guided to research present laws and viewpoints on gay marriages.

Lawrence Kriegel, A Loaded Question: What Is It about Americans and Guns? (p. 461)
(Cross-Chapter Connections: "Roots and Memories," "American Dreams and Creations," "Ways of Learning")

As they consider this essay, students once again confront an issue that polarizes readers: the question of gun control in America. Before reading Kriegel's argument, students should think about their initial encounter with or thoughts concerning guns. In addition, as a springboard for discussion, they might write their responses to the popular NRA slogan, "Guns don't kill, people do."

Although most of the arguments in Section 4, "Writing to Persuade" use legal cases and logic as the primary means of support, Kriegel's main persuasive strategy is the use of personal narrative. Students will almost certainly find this approach engaging and will discover themselves strongly affected by the incidents Kriegel includes.

As a reading exercise, you may want to have students keep a list of phrases and scenes that are most detailed and absorbing.

As students consider their list, they may note that Kriegel's piece offers a fine blend of narrative, exposition, and persuasion. His first paragraph demonstrates this blend, as he uses the first person, refers to himself as a child, and ends with a universal statement. Based on this first paragraph alone, you may want to have students consider the tone and purpose that they think will dominate this piece. Kriegel's tone is both personal and light, yet also concerned and assured.

After this first paragraph, the essay's organization goes something like this: Kriegel begins with a detailed narrative (par. 2–9). He switches to a blend of narrative and exposition in the following paragraphs (par. 10–16); he then combines persuasion with narration for the remainder of this essay.

As Kriegel explains, his first experience with a gun was during a "time I needed any triumph I could find, no matter how minor" (par. 10), a time when he felt vulnerable and powerless because of his long battle with the crippling effects of polio. However, his views on guns changed during the summer of 1977 when he realized the power and fear that come with the possession of a gun. He came to believe that a man who bears a gun "believes that power belongs not to the gun but to him" (par. 37).

Students should consider whether or not this narrative, personal approach is effectively persuasive. If any students previously upheld the right to own handguns, does Kriegel's piece convince them to rethink their views? Would it convince his friend in Maine? Might it convince an undecided reader—a person who had not yet formed a strong view on the gun-control issue? How does Kriegel, the man, come across to his audience? Certainly, many students will recognize the honesty and personal pain with which he writes. Through his first narrative, Kriegel reveals how fascinated he was with guns, how guns gave him a sense of power, a power he needed at the time because he was in a situation—wheelchair-bound—that caused him to be viewed by most of society as different and, almost certainly, as powerless.

However, his subsequent narratives—from a time when he was much older—reveal a mature, honest, balanced man. He writes of the beauty of guns and of the father-son ritual related to guns in America. He understands guns as a part of his country's history, and yet, when he comes face to face with a gun, he realizes the danger, as well as the seductive nature, of this weapon. Such a change-of-heart approach would probably be quite effective in convincing an undecided reader.

If students are asked to list publications that would possibly be interested in printing this essay, they may note that Kriegel's audience is primarily male. Other than brief references to female relatives and friends, the only woman mentioned is Jane Austen. All of the personal experiences involve male friends, strangers, or family members. Is Kriegel thus being sexist in his approach? Perhaps the author is simply being realistic. Guns are a traditional symbol of manhood, of "coming of age." Students could brainstorm to determine what the traditional symbols for women in this country are.

Students may also brainstorm for other possessions that fit into the fear/freedom category that Kriegel establishes. Fast cars, cigarettes, and alcohol might fall into this same pattern.

Kriegel's fine blend of classic allusions and contemporary images come together in his observation on the Furies and the weapons kept on display. Here he makes his main point, the pivot on which his whole argument revolves. To aid students in discovering his theme, have them experiment with the following phrase starter:

"Guns are dangerous because . . ." or

"Guns should be outlawed because . . . "

Completed sentences might address what the Furies symbolize: the craziness and irrationality that possess all humans from time to time and the potential that guns, in possession of the "Furies," have to be life-endangering weapons.

As an extension to this piece, students can experiment with the three writing aims that Kriegel incorporates in this piece. They can try to explain their position on this issue—or another controversial issues—by writing a letter, by writing a story that reveals their feelings on guns, or by doing research to determine the correlation between guns and killings in America.

Diane Ravitch, Multiculturalism: E Pluribus Plures (p. 471)
(Cross-Chapter Connections: "Ways of Learning," "Crossing Borders")

Although this piece fits logically with the "rights and responsibilities" theme, it is also an excellent semester "starter" that gets students in touch with the issues that unite the various chapters and selections in this text. You may want to begin with a discussion of the Latin phrase in Ravitch's title, which translates as "out of many, many," in contrast to the motto of the United States *E Pluribus Unum,* "out of many, one." What do the differences in these two phrases suggest? How does Ravitch's adaption suggest the questions raised by multiculturalism? What is multiculturalism, and do we need it? By writing and subsequently discussing the questions that precede this essay, students can identify and address their own preconceptions of, responses to, or experiences with multiculturalism.

After reading this piece, students' impressions of multiculturalism may be somewhat redefined. Encourage students to write about any change of thought they might have had between the pre- and post-reading discussions. Students need to be encouraged to change their minds, to suspend disbelief, so to speak, so that new learning can take place. Any students who have modified their thinking should also attempt to evaluate why this change took place. Was it because of class discussion? Something another student said? Was it a particular sentence, paragraph, or example from this essay?

In this piece, Ravitch sees "pluralistic multiculturalism" as an approach that "promotes a broader interpretation of the common American culture and seeks due recognition for the ways that the nation's many racial, ethnic, and cultural groups" have contributed to this country (par. 13). In other words, it is a coming together of all of the parts that create this fabric called America. "Particularistic multiculturalism," in contrast, promotes one specific group within the culture and is rooted in separatism. Ravitch cites the example of black extremism, which claims that black culture is the primary root of all American culture.

One who promotes "particularism" may answer back to Ravitch that one's individual culture is all that should matter. For example, devout Christians may believe that only Christian-based teachings are relevant to their children's upbringing and may see learning about other religions as irrelevant and invasive. Students can find further examples within the essay itself.

In contrast to those who demand particularism, yet also opposed to Ravitch's view, are those who see even the pluralistic approach to multiculturalism as a waste of time. Beliefs such as "Teach the classics" (meaning traditional, white, male Western writers) or

"Education should be limited to the basics, like reading, writing, and arithmetic" are not uncommon. Some critics feel that by adopting a multicultural approach, students receive bits of everything, without a solid overview of what these critics believe to be the unifying majority culture. You may want to stimulate discussion on this point by asking students questions such as these:

- What, if anything, does a first-grader gain or lose by learning about India?
- What, if anything, do students gain or lose when they read books by both male and female authors from various cultures, from many different time periods, from contrasting religious— or non-religious—backgrounds, from opposing political or philosophical schools of thought?
- What, if anything, do students gain or lose if they read only (or primarily) works that have traditionally been part of the dominant white male culture?

If nothing else, the reading and discussion of this essay should alert students to the controversies and choices available as they learn and grow, not only while they are in school but also throughout their lives. Do people really care about other cultures? Should we? Why or why not? These are questions that touch the heart of this text (and, most probably, the course in which students are reading this text). In addition to Ravitch's essay, students are urged to read other points of view on this complex issue. Similarly, they may also discover, via a questionnaire, the feelings toward multiculturalism on their own campus and even in their own families.

Leslie Marmon Silko, Lullaby (p. 484)
(Cross-Chapter Connections: "Parents and Children," "Roots and Memories," "American Dreams and Creations")

"Lullaby," a hauntingly poignant story that most students will remember for a long time to come, explores universal themes of innocence, of tragedy, and of endurance.

The heart of this story revolves around the old woman, Ayah, and her experiences as a mother and wife. The story moves between beautifully simple scenes and images of love and tragic moments. This contrast exists even within sentences. In the first paragraph alone, students can analyze each sentence and find an array of opposites:

- cottonwood — rough bark
- light of the snow — dark outline
- springtime — thin cows
- grass — chewed flat
- new grass — manure

Such close analysis will help students see this tug of war that continues throughout the entire story.

If they have keyed in to the idea of conflicts and opposites, then you might encourage them to complete the following phrase by using two opposing symbols. For example, "For me, life has been like . . ."

- living between summer and winter
- being planted and being weeded
- a desert and a snowfall
- a morning sunrise and an evening sunset

During Jimmy's birth and death, the world around Ayah changed. It became more populated, more industrialized. It went to war. It also became a world of legalities and parking lots, of cities, counties, and borders. Although the outside world changed, Ayah seemed to change little. Her life basically revolved around the cycles of nature. From the outside world, she learned not to trust those who came in cars, speaking English, and carrying papers for her to sign.

The relationship between Ayah and Chato is intriguing and complex. Although they lived together a good part of their lives, Chato is still a stranger to Ayah. Ask students if they believe this is an unusual occurrence. Do they think other people live together but do not know one another well? Perhaps what happened to Ayah and Chato is not so unique. Perhaps people fall into roles and routines; perhaps they stop talking about dreams or things they can no longer control. Perhaps at the heart of this story is the message of aloneness. If students have read Elizabeth Cady Stanton's piece on "The Solitude of Self" (text p. 421), now might be a good time to reflect on her message.

Ask students to compare the first time Ayah's children are taken from her and the last time they come to visit their mother. The initial separation is painful for obvious reasons. The last visit, seemingly emotionless, is perhaps even more painful. Now Ayah realizes she has lost her children forever, and the children will never know—and will never want to know—the life they once lived. Did the government really do the children a favor? What might they have gained? Lost?

Although this piece is fiction, many students will see that the issues of rights and responsibility it raises are very real. Who has the right to take children away? Who is responsible for defining another's happiness? What is more important: a "good" life—i.e., a nice home, clothes, education—or a whole family?

Students are invited to cast their own characters for this short story. In addition, you may want to invite students to act out a chosen scene from this piece and write the dialogue that Silko omits. You may also ask students to consider doing a soliloquy from any one of the characters' point of view.

Gwendolyn Brooks, The Mother (p. 497)
(Cross-Chapter Connections: "Roots and Memories," "Parents and Children")

Like the prereading suggestions for "Lullaby" (text p. 484), the prereading topics for "The Mother" urge students to use their journals as a way of working through a painful experience.

Most students will have little trouble at least capturing the essence of this poem. The title, as many will see, suggests that this piece is being written by and primarily for "The Mother." She has to come to terms with her past; she has to achieve her own sense of closure, or at least try to make sense of it all.

Brooks chooses to talk with the reader by using the second person "you" in the first stanza before moving to "I" in the second and subsequent stanzas. This approach suggests an attempt to establish common ground and to delay the reader's judgment. The use of "you" also asks the reader to put him or herself in the position of the speaker.

There are many graphic and painful images in this poem. The descriptions of the fetuses and their actions may be most disturbing. Some students may feel quite angry as they contemplate these images. The question that seems to emerge at this point of discussion is, "If this woman was so sensitive to these babies, how could she?" When she says she was not "deliberate," what does she mean? Did she really know what she was doing? Or did she feel she had a choice? Did she have a choice? These are the questions that will keep students thoughtful for a good part of your class period. During these discussions, remember to ask students for references to the text. If they see the decision to abort as a "crime," whose "crime" might it have been, other than the mother's? Does the speaker say? What can students infer from studying the images in the poem?

What is it that the speaker in the poem really hopes to achieve? Students' responses to this question will vary, and certainly there are many possibilities. Perhaps the mother seeks forgiveness—but from whom? And for what? The tone is both sad and honest. Perhaps the mother wants to explain to others the pain and complexity of choosing abortion. Perhaps the speaker wants to be able to forgive herself. Perhaps the speaker wants to come to her own understanding of the contradictions of her life. Certainly, in the final shift to "you," which now apparently refers to her unborn children, the notions of seeking forgiveness or understanding are quite strong.

If students have also read Silko's "Lullaby" (text p. 484), a comparison here would enrich appreciation of both pieces of literature. Questions to foster comparisons will help students draw thoughtful conclusions:

- What are the settings for each woman? What is her world like?
- What type of person is she?
- How does she feel about her children?
- What does she do to or for her children?
- Why does she lose her children?
- Is she able to make good choices?
- Does she have any support, or is she alone?

In addition to comparing two pieces of literature, students may choose to write an extended definition of what a good mother is, synthesizing the selections they have read along with their own experiences.

READINGS: QUESTIONS OF LANGUAGE

Photographs and Previews (pp. 496–498)
Suggestions for Writing

Photographs

1. From the look on the woman's face to the left of the man, does she appear to be a demonstrator or a bystander?
    What do you think the demonstrators in this scene are demonstrating for (or against)?

2. In what ways do the three banners reflect two different, but equal cultures?
    If you look closely, you can see that the three children holding the banner all have different expressions. Explain the differences and the significance of these contrasting expressions.

3. From this photograph, can you tell which woman is learning a language and which one is teaching it?
    Do the women understand one another? Why or why not?

Previews

1. From these quotations, what conclusions can you draw about the purposes of language?

2. In one way or another, these five quotations relate to educational experiences. What is it about language that schools should—or should not—teach?

Cross-Reference List: Alternative Selections for "Questions of Language"

Selection	Text Page
Learning to Read and Write	151
The Loudest Voice (fiction)	194
Shanghai Blues	293
The Arabs' Image	584

Angelo Gonzales, Bilingual Education: The Key to Basic Skills (p. 499)
(Cross-Chapter Connections: "Ways of Learning," "Crossing Borders")

This essay, combined with Richard Rodriguez's piece (text p. 503), allows students to grasp reasonable arguments both for and against bilingual education in America. Students can best appreciate this issue if they complete both of the prereading topics. Through these topics, students can imagine themselves in the same situation as the student whose first language is not English; they can also recall a time when learning failed them—or they failed to learn.

As students read this essay, you may suggest they list the statements with which (1) they strongly agree, (2) they strongly disagree, or (3) they neither agree nor disagree and identify their reasons for these responses. This process can lead to a discussion of whether or not Gonzales is, in general, logical and reasonable.

After reading this selection, students are asked to write a one-sentence summary of the author's main point. If several students write their sentences on the board, or if students compare summaries in small groups, they will be able to see which statements include the reader's opinion, which statements are only partially true, which statements deal only with peripheral issues or include too many details, and which statements are, indeed, effective summaries. Here is a list of possible examples:

- In this piece, Gonzales thinks that everyone should speak his or her native language in class and I don't think that's right.

- Gonzales believes that children cannot learn unless they are taught in their native language.

- In this piece, Gonzales deals with the issue of bilingual education.

- In a reasonable manner, Gonzales argues that since understanding the basic skill of reading is essential to success in education, language-minority children ought to be taught to read in their native languages in our public schools.

Most students would agree that the last example provides the most complete and accurate one-sentence summary of this article.

A review of Gonzales's sources reveals the following:

- New York City Report on Bilingual Services, 1982–83 (par. 3)

- Henji Hakuta's study at Yale University (no date given) (par. 4)
- Jim Cummins, from Ontario Institute for Studies in Education (no date given) (par. 5)
- Three national data bases (no date given) (par 5)
- Educational Priorities panel (par. 9)

Consider asking students which source they feel is most reliable and most valid. If they choose either one of the first two sources, ask further: Would these sources be impartial as far as bilingual education goes? The third source is questionable. Who is Jim Cummins and why might his opinion matter? The last two seem reliable. However, ask students to reread the conclusions and recommendations based on these sources. The three national data bases refer to high school students; in this piece, Gonzales is arguing for "children." The last source doesn't substantiate Gonzales's view of same-language teaching; it only states that more children are in need of services.

In this argument, Gonzales chooses an appeal primarily to reason, as opposed to emotions or ethics. From the biographical information, students should recognize that the author is an advocate for Hispanics and their organizations. Therefore, an approach to reason makes his voice less biased, more fair-minded. His audience might very well be voters whose opinions can make a difference. Do students think this appeal is the most effective? Considering Gonzales's position, most should agree that it is.

Question No. 4 asks students to see themselves as teachers. You may first want to ask students if they have had friendships with people who did not speak the same language. How did they go about communicating? What seemed the best way to understand one another? Students who are interested in education may offer many suggestions to nurture bilingual children in their classrooms; whatever the suggestions may be, the following principle seems essential: Give bilingual children time; be patient; never ridicule students for any attempts at speaking the English language.

Gonzales states his basic claim in the opening line: "a child cannot learn unless taught through the language he speaks and understands." Based on this premise and the premise that all children in this country are guaranteed the right to learn, Gonzales draws the conclusion that language-minority students have the right to an effective, bilingual education.

Students may raise the following issues to counter Gonzales's claims. First of all, children can learn despite a language barrier. The learning may just be slower. In fact, in the long run, many educators believe the "immersion" approach is more beneficial. Secondly, our country does guarantee every citizen a free education, but it does not guarantee a free and individualized education program. Thirdly, students could argue for a middle ground. Teach reading in a native language; teach other subjects in English.

In order to bring this argument to life, consider contacting various students from your school who have experienced either a bilingual or an immersion-type learning program in this country's public schools. This panel of experts could certainly give students much to think about concerning the complexity of language and learning.

Richard Rodriguez, Bilingual Education: Outdated and Unrealistic (p. 503)
(Cross-Chapter Connections: "Ways of Learning," "Crossing Borders")

To expose students to two sides of the same issue, have them read this essay and the Gonzales essay (text p. 499) as complementary pieces. By contrasting these two pieces, students will be able to see how the authors compare on theme, purpose, audience, appeal, tone, and style.

The difference in theme is clear. Gonzales believes students learn better when they have access to their own language. Rodriguez not only doubts this approach, but also believes that in many ways bilingual education puts an extra burden on the child, both in and out of school (Question No. 1).

Rodriguez uses primarily ethical and emotional appeals. He appeals to the audience's sense of right and wrong (ethical appeal) when he cites memory and incidents of child abuse. His ending uses this same appeal as well. When he recalls his own childhood, the appeal is clearly emotional. He writes, "I was that child!" (par. 16) and goes on to explain how he survived and eventually thrived in the English-only classroom.

Rodriguez discounts any studies done on bilingual education because he feels the issue goes beyond the schoolyard. In addition, he feels that facts and figures can show only one part of the picture.

Students should be able to come up with their own examples of how easily facts can be skewed.

Both Gonzales and Rodriguez want Hispanic children to learn. However, what they want them to learn is at the heart of this dispute. Gonzales wants Hispanics to learn their own language first and to feel secure in their culture, before venturing out. Rodriguez wants children to learn as he did. He believes each child must go out and use the language of the dominant culture, seeing the acquisition of this language as the essential link to the society in which he or she must live. Simply put, Gonzales seems to advocate a cultural respect, whereas Rodriguez advocates a pragmatic course for success in the world of the dominant culture. Students might also note that Rodriguez not only advocates immersion in the dominant culture's language at school; in addition, he urges that families give up speaking their own language to their children. The child, then, in Rodriguez's ideal learning situation does not become bilingual but rather gives up his or her first language entirely.

This highly complex issue lends itself well to an in-class debate. As students plan the debate, developing their own arguments, appeals, and support, you might address the notion of fair-mindedness in an argument. The most effective argument usually concedes at least one possible "truth" on the side of the opposition. (For example, through his examples, Rodriguez acknowledges the pain and humiliation that language-minority students often feel.)

In addition to the Extended Thinking suggestions, which encourage students to research how other countries deal with bilingual education, the more involved students may want to read *Savage Inequalities* by Jonathan Kozol. Among other things, this recent book describes how many students in America are denied an effective education, with most innovative and acclaimed programs being available only to those who already come from privileged backgrounds.

Barbara Lawrence, Four-Letter Words Can Hurt You (p. 507)
(Cross-Chapter Connections: "Roots and Memories," "Men and Women")

Because both Gloria Naylor (text p. 520) and Lawrence deal with a similar issue—the power of words—consider having students read these two essays for comparison. The prereading suggestions concerning obscene words can apply to either one of these essays.

To begin, you may want students to think about whether obscene words do often reflect an underlying hatred and fear of women. If these words are accepted as a reasonable part of our language, does this acceptance signal a willingness to ignore the implications? Consider, for instance, how many more taboo words refer to women or to actions that hurt women than to men. Although students will find acceptance of four-letter words common (all they have to do is look to records, television shows, and films to back up their point), many will also recognize the power of sexual slang that is prevalent today (again, a review of recordings, television shows, and films should back up this point).

Lawrence bases her arguments on the meaning behind the words—the original intentions and functions of the words. She cites Latin roots (par. 4) and goes on to explain the literal implications of a word (example: "screw," par. 4). Lawrence's examples are quite effective; note particularly words whose functions are graphically painful, especially for women ("screw," "bang").

Some of the most well-known four-letter words are not written in this piece, and students should wonder why Lawrence feels free to include ethnic terms but not these "bodily function" words. Considering the piece was written two decades ago, her reason may have been that such words might have been censored at the time. Another reason Lawrence only describes the words is to draw in her audience. She knows very well that her readers know the words she is speaking of, whether she specifically states them or not.

Question No. 4 invites students to play the devil's advocate with this argument. It also allows them to counterattack Lawrence on the issue of free speech and censorship. If you want to hold a formal debate on this issue, encourage students to research Supreme Court decisions on free speech in relation to public school publications. This process allows them to analyze and evaluate a higher court's ruling and viewpoints on a similar issue.

Robin Lakoff, Talking Like a Lady (p. 510)
(Cross-Chapter Connections: "Men and Women," "Crossing Borders")

In addition to writing about the connotations that words carry, Lakoff's essay also contends that the patterns of language and the intonations within male-female conversations parallel the dominant-subservient relationships between the two sexes.

Lakoff states her main point at the beginning of paragraph 3: "This lexical disparity reflects a social inequity in the position of women." To test Lakoff's thesis, consider asking students to observe discussion in several of their other classes and to note examples that support or challenge her contention.

As students read and reflect on any argument, they should become increasingly aware of the rhetorical strategies available to the writer. You might note that the power of some of these strategies exists mainly because most people do not stop to think about *how* an idea is being presented to them, but simply respond to what they believe they are hearing. Question No. 2 provides a list of quotations and asks students to discern between fact and opinion. The presence of qualifying words becomes important here, and, given a little time and encouragement, most students will become proficient at recognizing these terms. For example, the following quotations contain qualifiers that keep the statement from being an absolute: **A** ("tends to") and **D** ("supposedly"). Clever debaters often use such internal qualifiers because they recognize that while the statement is literally arbitrary, many members of an audience will hear it—and accept it—as absolute. To discover examples, have students check a few advertisements or political speeches.

To answer Question No. 3, students should stop and think about what some readers will believe the two pairs mentioned have in common. Women and hippies: open to change, radical, idealistic, a bit naive, outside of the power circle, ridiculed! Women and the British aristocrats: cultured, proper, mannerly, concerned with appearance and protocol, treated to the easy life, the life of watching but not doing. Women and academic men: thinkers but not workers, idealistic, outside of the power circle in the "real" world (business/politics/ military). Students may, of course, come up with many other possible similarities as well.

In this essay, Lakoff's primary aim seems to be making an argument for her view of language. She does not directly urge any action or change of thought. However, readers who watch for connotation and who consider the last paragraph with special care will probably conclude that Lakoff would like to see women become more assertive, more direct in their conversations with men.

Again, if students take the time to analyze just one paragraph from this piece, they should form some impression of the author herself. What does she think of her audience? How does she treat her audience? How does she present herself? How does she treat her subject? The best question to ask is, of course, Does she "speak" in this piece as she claims most women speak? Is she carefully polite? Does she express strong opinions, or is she tentative? How does she use figurative adjectives (see, for instance, par. 9)? Does she seem confident in her knowledge, or is she raising questions? Does she commit herself, or does she seem reluctant to state her opinion?

Gloria Naylor, A Question of Language (p. 520)
(Cross-Chapter Connections: "Roots and Memories," "Crossing Borders")

Like Rodriguez (text p. 503) and Jones (text p. 532) in this section, Naylor includes her personal experience as a way to draw inferences on how much spoken language affects the way we feel and the way we think. Students are asked to consider their own experiences with words before reading this piece. Some students may be open to sharing their list of "forbidden" words, and, if so, such an informal discussion will further connect the student to Naylor's main points as well as to her process of presenting her argument.

If, as Naylor writes, language is the subject of her opening narrative, what is the major conflict this story suggests? You might ask students if the author as a young girl took offense with what the third-grade boy said to her. They should recognize that while the word *nigger* in itself, didn't offend the author, how and why the boy said it caused her pain. Naylor's main point, then, might be expressed like this: The spoken word's power stems from undeniable intention as well as unmistakable emphasis on the part of the speaker. In other words, the real meaning in spoken language is found not in the words themselves, but in the definition these words are given by the speaker's beliefs and values.

To further explain her point, Naylor cites several instances when she heard the word *nigger* and was not offended. In general, when it was used by other black people, the word took on a neutral or positive meaning. It was a term used to indicate love ("my nigger"), as well as to reveal pride ("Don't mess with a nigger"). In her own community, Naylor wasn't puzzled, hurt, or angered by the word *nigger*, because the meaning conveyed by the beliefs and values of those who used it was not pejorative or demeaning.

However, when the term was used by an outsider, it took on derogatory connotations. The analogy can perhaps be made that within a family people have the right to tease one another. However, when someone outside of the family uses the same teasing term, it takes on a different meaning. The term isn't accepted as readily because the outsider doesn't really understand or belong to the workings of the family.

What does a parent say to a child who has been verbally attacked by another child? Consider asking two volunteers to role-play a possible conversation between the young Naylor and her mother or father as they discuss what has happened at school that day. Students observing the role playing should pay special attention to the words that the two speakers emphasize.

As an extended activity, students can conduct a survey to discover the subtle connotations of certain "loaded" words. Suggest that students have any respondents use words in sentences as well as give definitions so that the true connotations can be unraveled.

Peter Farb, Linguistic Chauvinism (p. 524)
(Cross-Chapter Connections: "Roots and Memories," "Ways of Learning," "Crossing Borders")

Prior to reading this piece, students should think about the basic purposes of language. Asking students to see language as creating a bond between a speaker and an audience encourages them to recognize how flexible language can be, depending on the relationship between the two people speaking. In addition, students may enjoy sharing family "words." Certainly euphemisms for words such as *death* and *sex* will vary among students' family backgrounds.

You might take this opportunity to give a short lesson in etymology. Many students will not know the original meaning and derivation of *chauvinism*, a word that dates back to the Napoleonic empire. Nicolas Chauvin of Rochefort, a soldier of the First Republic and Empire, demonstrated extreme patriotism and attachment to Napoleon and to the country he represented. Chauvin's comrades ridiculed him for this blind, unreasoning pride, calling those who shared his unthinking devotion to France "chauvinists."

The term has since been applied to those who insist on believing their own characteristics superior to those of anyone else. Some students may associate the term *chauvinism* with the women's movement of the sixties. Men were first termed "chauvinists" in America during this era, and the meaning needed little interpretation. A male chauvinist, as most will know, was a bully, a man who believed he was better than women based solely on his sex; a man who had little, if any, respect for women; a man who was blind and failed to recognize women's desire and right to be treated as equals. The term's meaning is exactly the same when it comes to language. A linguistic chauvinist is one who doesn't respect another person's language, believes in the superiority of his or her language, has little or no respect for anyone else's way of communicating, thinks there is only one way—the white American English way—of speaking properly.

As Farb points out, black English is a highly structured language in its own right, as opposed to an error-ridden version of white English. Although the differences are many, Farb concentrates on the differences in vowel sounds, verb tenses, and grammar structures between white and black English. Actually, Farb says, black English is more precise as far as time and repetition of an action.

Clearly Farb is an expert in his field. In fact, some students may need help understanding his more complex points. Perhaps reading aloud the examples Farb gives on vowel sounds and verb phrases will help most students at least hear the differences. Farb probably envisions his audience as intelligent, educated people who are not linguistic experts but who do have interest in language issues. If students are really drawn into this subject, consider inviting a linguistic scholar into the classroom as a guest speaker so that the students can learn even more about the history of language.

Although many students will see the part that language plays in learning acquisition, students should think beyond the text. What other factors might interfere with a child's learning process? In a whole-class brainstorming session, students could come up with a variety of social issues that affect learning: family structure, poverty, sickness, disillusionment, and so on. Whether or not these factors are more important than language is subject to debate. However, some students may feel that even when language isn't a barrier, many inner-city children don't learn because of being hungry or tired or demoralized.

Students should search through the text to find evidence Farb gives to back up his claim that if a language isn't used it will die. For support, he offers the fact that since 1930, census figures show "fewer Americans claim a non-English mother tongue." As support, this statement is obviously flawed. Farb's census figure may be true, but he does not give any historical data to back up his claim that the decline of non-English speakers has resulted from lack of practice of a different first language.

In the first two-thirds of this essay, Farb adopts a reasonable approach to his topic. He cites dates, names, countries, historical events, and scholarly research. However, when he addresses the issue of whether or not "the black child survives the trauma of school," he subtly adopts an ethical tone and appeals to the audience's sense of right and wrong. Some students may recognize the effectiveness of starting out logically and moving to an ethical appeal in the course of an argument. You might ask them to gather examples from speeches they have heard on television or in their communities.

Again, students are invited to debate the issue of black language in the public schools. During this debate, however, students should refer to Farb's piece, either for support or rebuttal of any point they wish to make.

Should you make the option of analyzing a rap song available to your class, consider having students present their musical choices as well as their analyses to the entire class.

Rachel L. Jones, What's Wrong with Black English? (p. 532)
(Cross-Chapter Connections: "Roots and Memories," "Crossing Borders")

While Farb, a professor of linguistics, contends that black English is a language in its own right (text p. 524), a black student, Rachel Jones, finds that while dialects should be respected, black people should also know and speak "white English" in certain circumstances. Jones then answers affirmatively the question students are asked to consider by the prereading topics: Should we change our way of speaking, depending on the audience?

If students discuss their responses to this question, many will find that they may speak to friends one way, while addressing casual acquaintances or elderly relatives in other ways. The harder question to answer is this: Why do we change our ways of speaking? Shouldn't we be one way to all people? These questions should move the discussion beyond surface reactions to deeper thinking. Are we being phony or are we being appropriate?

Jones sees black English as appropriate "around family and friends" (par. 6). However, she contends that language should connect people—not separate them. Thus, she advocates less dependence "on a dialect that excludes [black people] from full participation in the world we live in" (last paragraph).

Perhaps because Jones is a college student, some readers may find her ideas a bit "ivory towerish," out of touch with the way things really are. After all, as a sophomore at Southern Illinois University, chances are that, as a black, she is in the minority. To succeed, she must adhere to the rules of the game, so to speak. In a debate with Farb (text p. 524), Jones might very well argue that, at the very least, black students should know both languages. However, as her ending comment indicates ("I don't think I talk white, I think I talk right"), she would not promote the acceptance of black English in or out of the classroom for young students.

By including her family's background (par. 2), Jones seeks to show that she does not come from a privileged background. As she says, her life was "only slightly better than poverty." She probably includes this detail to suggest that she stands connected to all black people, whether they live in poverty or affluence. She recognizes the importance of establishing common ground with her audience.

Jones sees herself excluded more from her black culture than from white culture because of her language patterns. As she says, "Because of the way I talk, some of my black peers look at me sideways and ask, 'Why do you talk like you're white?'" (par. 2). Now is the prime time to ask students the following question: Does the way in which people use language exclude or include them in certain groups? Is language an important a sign of one's culture?

Question No. 5 invites speculation on how our reading diets affect our inner thoughts and our language patterns. Students might consider the following questions: If Jones had attended an all-black school, one that stressed from the beginning the importance and validity of "black English," would her ideas be different from those she now holds? If she had attended an all-white school that followed a traditional curriculm would she have been exposed to black writers or to any type of dialect? Perhaps because most students are exposed primarily to mainstream American authors where characters who speak in dialect are generally regarded as comic, few students see the need for or the importance of retaining a dialect.

Perhaps one of Jones's strongest points comes in the section in which she addresses the language that most influential black people use. She cites two of the most honored black leaders—Malcolm X and Martin Luther King—as well as modern black writers. She also includes present-day black politicians from Atlanta to Texas. It may be interesting to ask if any students could counterattack her argument here. Can they cite any black leaders who use black English? At this point, you might consider bringing in a videotape of current black leaders such as Jesse Jackson and Barbara Jordan.

As a counterargument to Jones's examples, some students may suggest that if we all received a multicultural education, beginning with nursery school, then dialects would be valued and would not separate people as much as they do today. Students may also prefer to promote the "time and place" philosophy instead of insisting, as Jones does at the end, that there is a "right" way to speak —a "right" way that must always follow the majority way.

Gish Jen, What Means Switch (p. 536)
(Cross-Chapter Connections: "Ways of Learning," "Men and Women," "Crossing Borders")

Most students, whether male, female, traditional-age freshmen, or returning adults, will find this short story among their favorites in the text. Author Gish Jen writes with remarkable clarity and honesty as she describes the dilemmas of two young people faced with conflicting pressures from their school, their classmates, their families, and their cultures. Although the major conflict in this piece relates to the differences between a Chinese-American and a newly arrived Japanese student, many students will also recognize the universal theme of trying to fit in while trying to become an independent person.

If students share their initial responses to this story, they are apt to see the levels of conflicts within it. Some may respond to the clique community in junior high school; some may connect with the family relationships; some will identify with the way adolescents change in order to fit in. Many will also recognize the myth in the adage "Love conquers all."

Although Mona belongs to parts of various cultures in this piece (the Asian-American culture, Catholic-American culture, the Asian culture, the American culture, the Jewish-American culture), the primary culture to which she belongs is the culture of mainstream American adolescence. At this point in her life, she has adopted all of the concerns, thoughts, and actions appropriate to this age group. She thinks in terms of status symbols ("Isn't it better to be beautiful and rich than ugly and poor?"). Support for this reading can be found throughout this story, especially in the following paragraphs: 4–14, 37–58, 93–94, 133–156, 161–185, 198–end.

The basic difference between Mona and her mother is symbolized by the mother's secure grounding in her Chinese heritage. As a matter of fact, in this piece, Mona's mother is the one minor character who has a sense of balance between her heritage and her new country. She understands the importance of her Chinese culture, yet she also recognizes the necessity of becoming part of the place where she now lives. She sees her heritage slipping away the longer she stays in America (example: she cannot remember all of the ancient Chinese characters when she is writing).

Mona and her friends seem similar. They all are concerned with appearances and with being popular. They know the best places to shop, the best movies to see, the best foods to eat. When Sherman comes into the picture, however, Mona gradually changes. At first, she is anxious to share her experiences with her girl friends. However, as her feelings for Sherman begin to deepen, she talks (or brags) less about this relationship with her friends. The relationship has moved beyond the "in thing to do" and affects her as an individual. Mona and Sherman are similar insofar as they are both young and in love. What teachers and classmates see as a similarity—Mona's and Sherman's

Asian heritage—is, of course, at the heart of their differences. Mona is, essentially, an American teenager. Sherman is a Japanese teenager. In addition, of course, Mona's and Sherman's families are acutely aware—as her peers and teachers are not—of the differences (and long-standing conflicts) between Japan and China.

The big question is found in the title of this piece. Is it possible for someone to switch cultures? Can someone grounded in one faith totally adopt and become a person of another faith? Can any individual completely ignore his or her nationality or national origins? Students should discuss this issue based on their own experiences and the experiences of those they know.

When Mona first notices Sherman, she sees him through the eyes of a typical American teenager. She notices his looks and the type of notebook he is carrying. Basically, she notices only how different he is from all the others in her group. However, when the other students start to look up to Sherman as a judo expert, Mona starts to look up to him too. It might be "cool" to like him. In other words, like most teenagers, Mona has to first decide whether or not the other kids accept Sherman before she can admit that she likes him too. This fact reinforces the notion that her main culture is that of American adolescence.

Most students should recognize that, besides cultural differences, Mona and Sherman may have trouble communicating simply because they are of different sexes. As Mona says, the deeper their feelings become for each other, the more they "reach a point where we can hardly talk at all."

In contrast to the typical American family, the relationships within Sherman's family are more private and more exclusive. Sherman's father is assigned a clearly defined role, while his mother plays an equally clearly defined, yet distinctly different, role. They also have a strong sense of pride in their country and their history. In addition to this, respect for the family hierarchy takes precedence over the individual's feelings or desires. In Mona's Chinese-American family, her parents seem less inclined to tell her what to do; in turn, she feels less inclined to follow their advice or to take an interest in the stories of their past.

The final paragraph is loaded with bittersweet images suggesting just how painful finding a "goodness of fit" can be. The churned-up yard symbolizes both Mona's feelings and her relationship with

Sherman. What looked set on the outside was really quite fragile in reality. In between all the potential life, innocence, and beauty (the irises and lilies of the valley) run two mud tracks—the tracks, literally, of two cultures conflicting: the American car and the Japanese driver. In addition to this, the fact that Mona's father has to work again to replant may suggest how hard it is to take root in another country.

Final symbols in this paragraph include the blood and the brick wall. The blood may stand for both the passion and the pain that Mona has experienced, while the brick wall, among other things, stands as a final reminder that barriers between cultures take a very long time to break down.

Kitty Tsui, Don't Let Them Chip Away at Our Language (p. 551) (Cross-Chapter Connections: "Roots and Memories," "American Dreams and Creations," "Crossing Borders")

As the title indicates, the speaker contends that language belongs to those who use it. The conflict, of course, is found in the words "Them," which connotes faceless strangers, and "Chip," which connotes a constant, irritating erosion.

Tsui's intentional use of lower-case letters may have several effects on the audience. First, students may get the feeling of smallness, of shyness, from this technique. Certainly this interpretation fits with the way the speaker and her family feel in relation to the language majority in America. The lower-case letters may also give students the feeling of humility or of independence. Any (and all) of these interpretations can be defended by citing details from the poem.

The grandmother's words can be categorized under the following titles:

> Surface relationships (l. 1, 2)
>
> Symbols of American hospitality (l. 12–17)
>
> Commercialization (l. 24–31).

Together, these words indicate that the grandmother had formed few close ties, but still accepted parts of the American dream, at least as she saw that dream reflected on her television. These examples suggest that she is excluded from companionship and the realities of mainstream America.

Tsui includes the history of the Chinese in America to show the contributions this nationality has made to the American culture. The first settlers were instrumental in bringing new products to America and in bringing American goods to those outside of the country. In addition to this, they contributed to the basic quality of life for mainstream Americans, often in the role of severely exploited and mistreated laborers: They cooked the food, sewed the clothes, built the roads, forged the way so that East could meet West (note the irony in this last detail). The speaker insists that readers notice the contribution of Chinese workers to the health and wealth of America.

The speaker in the poem ends with a plea urging all people to respect other cultures and their languages. In contrast to this plea, lines 39–41 sound strong, courageous, and challenging ("we're no longer/going to let them/chip away at our language"). Students should think about why the tone changes so drastically between the middle and the end—possibly the determination comes from the speaker's increasing recognition that oppression will not stop without serious and even confrontational resistance.

READINGS: CROSSING BORDERS

Photographs and Previews (pp. 556–558)
Suggestions for Writing

Photographs

1.   When, where, and why do you think this gathering is taking place? What details in this scene reveal two distinct cultures?

2.   Hold this picture at arm's length. Without focusing in on details, what impression do you get?
Why is it that athletes can bring a whole world together?

3.   Under what circumstances might these two people have been brought together?
If you could be present during this scene, about what subjects might you hear these two people talking?

Previews

1. From these quotations, what would you say is at the heart of creating hostile borders between people and nations?

2. When can borders actually serve to unite people?

Cross-Reference List: Alternative Selections for "Crossing Borders"

Alice Bloom, On a Greek Holiday (p. 559)
(Cross-Chapter Connections: "Arriving," "Ways of Learning")

Tourists usually have one of the following options: traveling in comfort or roughing it. According to this author, the best approach is by way of the back roads of another country. When students write about their choices, however, they may find that initially, at least, vacationing means anything but rubbing elbows with the local folks. However, with her beautiful details and photographic scenes, Bloom just may convince even the most reluctant of explorers that an unconventional journey to another land is a most satisfying way of taking an inner journey to a new view of ourselves.

Bloom's point in this piece is quite obvious. If Americans dare to "spend as little as possible" (par. 29) in a foreign country, if they dare to walk back roads and speak the native language, they will really experience and know what another culture is like. Bloom admits that the comforts of a Hilton are tempting, but the rewards, she insists, are few.

In the beginning of this piece, Bloom spends a great deal of space describing typical travel procedures and posters (par. 2–5). If students look closely, they will see that the details on the posters can be categorized under one topic: play. The landscapes are impeccable, the natives bright and friendly, and the shopping unmatched. By saying that the natives in these advertisements look like "character dolls" (par. 5), Bloom implies that the American view of vacationing in a foreign land is somewhat childish, somewhat plastic, and certainly stereotyped—expecting people who live in other countries to dress in costumes that have probably not been customary for many decades, perhaps even centuries.

Students should have little trouble recognizing the implications of Bloom's comparison of the profiles of the Greek woman and the young blond tourist. The Greek woman (par. 16) appears to be a woman of substance—deep, humorous, wise, purposeful, whole. The American tourist, on the other hand, looks and acts like an ad out of a cheap magazine. Bloom writes that "she looks like she couldn't dress a doll without having a fit of sulks and throwing it down in a tantrum" (par. 17). Ask students what this image means, and most will see that this tourist can tolerate only that which comes easily. As Bloom clarifies, she may look beautiful, but "presence, she has not" (par. 17).

By now, students should see that Bloom has definite opinions of American tourists, and she doesn't mind a bit stating her views clearly. Is Bloom being fair by characterizing this tourist as artificial, spoiled, indulged? At this point, you might ask students to draw on their own experiences. Ask students who have traveled to other countries to share their experiences. What did they discover about American tourists? What did they discover about themselves as tourists?

When Bloom talks of the relationship between simplicity and the complex life, she is really talking about the life of substance, the life of the Greek woman. From the simple, she ascertains, we learn about the connectedness, the roots, the complexity of life in general. From the simple pieces, we can see the whole plan. However, since most Americans, according to Bloom, just depend on buying everything, they are "removed from the rich, complete life of that place" (par. 27).

Although students' answers will vary as to how Bloom would define happiness, most should see that the author's definition must be connected somehow to the image of the Greek woman. Perhaps to Bloom, a happy person is one who "sees and understands" the deeper mysteries of life. It is the person who "stops thinking of the good life strictly in terms of goods, services, and various rights" (par. 19). Perhaps happiness is experiencing and celebrating the simple pleasures and routines in our lives. If so, you might ask students: Are most Americans happy, according to such definitions?

In conclusion, Bloom believes that Americans aim for familiar and convenient surroundings in foreign places because, basically, they are spoiled, lazy, and afraid of "the unfamiliar and the uncomfortable" (par. 28). Again, students should feel free to disagree with the author on this point. After all, her only support for this argument is what she has seen in her own travels. You may want to direct students back to their prereading answers: How did they say they would spend their time? If they did say they would lounge on at an ocean resort, sipping exotic drinks the whole time, how would they respond to Bloom? What are the advantages of the "blond tourist" approach?

As extended activity possibilities, students can interview others in order to discover if Bloom's assessment seems to be on target. In addition to this, students may also want to write their own richly detailed descriptions of a place they have visited.

Aryeh Neier, Pornography Here and Abroad (p. 570)
(Cross-Chapter Connections: "Men and Women," "Ways of Learning")

If possible, allow a good part of the class period before students read Neier's argument to discuss the issue of pornography. Neier's essay is quite short, and its strength is in its ability to urge students to question an issue on their own. Where do they stand on this issue? Why do they think the way they do? What is the basis for their beliefs? To move to possible causes and effects, ask students why people might subscribe to pornographic materials. In addition, what might be the effects of such publications on a viewer?

Such a discussion, controversial as it may be, may show students that in a sound argument, the speaker must support any distinctions that are pertinent. For example, if students come to the conclusion that materials that misuse children are pornographic, then they have to support their differentiation between children and, say, adolescents. Such exact reasoning is not always easy.

Unlike Bloom (text pp. 559), whose stance was quite clear, students may have to draw on inferential thinking in order to adequately summarize Neier's point. They will have to think in terms of his declared statements and proceed logically. What does the author state?

- In America one finds a great deal of pornography as well as hostility and violence against women.
- In repressive countries, there is virtually no pornography, but much sexual repression and violence.
- One conclusion: Pornography has little to do with sexual violence and aggression.
- Claim: The more you have of something, the less satisfying it is.
- Americans are spoiled and need to feel satisfied, so even though pornography is not satisfying, they have to try to get more and more in order to feel satisfied.
- Main conclusion: The rage over pornography in the United States is much ado about nothing. (In the author's own words, "pornography is really not very important" [par. 1].)

Now that students have isolated Neier's main points, they should be able to judge them in terms of logic. Is it true—the more you have of something the less satisfying it is? Examples from students' own lives in terms of food, clothing, and so on, may be helpful here.

A tougher analysis involves Neier's reasoning concerning pornography and violence against women. Neier implies that pornography neither causes nor aggravates sexual violence. Can students provide any facts to the contrary? Are the sources that Neier uses sufficient? What else could he use to provide a stronger argument?

Besides reflecting a society that is "spoiled by too much of everything," students should think about what else pornography reflects about American society. To do this, they may want to use Neier's contrasting groups: repressive countries and America. Of course, the question still remains as to whether or not conclusions are legitimate. Students could also look to trends within America and see if there may be a correlation between a specific trend (rise in divorces) and pornography. As most students will discover, to pinpoint a direct cause-effect theory is a virtual impossibility except in a scientifically controlled experiment.

For Extended Thinking and Research activities, students are directed to research other countries as well as other viewpoints on this subject. In addition to this, students may choose to write a dialogue between Bloom and Neier as to what really is a source of satisfaction and happiness in America today.

Martin Esslin, Beyond the Wasteland: What American TV Can Learn from the BBC (p. 572)
(Cross-Chapter Connections: "American Dreams and Creations," "Rights and Responsibilities," "Ways of Learning")

Before reading this essay, students should take time to get in touch with the ways media affect them as individuals. Further, they should also think of their preferences in terms of the majority. What some students may uncover here is one of Esslin's main points: By depending on commercialism, American television cannot address the needs of special interests or the arts.

Although both Bloom and Neier depend primarily on general consensus and their own experiences to support their arguments, Esslin devotes nearly half of his argument to television's historical base in both countries. Thus, when he gets to his major points, he and his audience share a mutual wealth of knowledge. Certainly most students will feel they've gained new insights regarding the roots of this powerful industry.

The differences Esslin sets forth are many. In order to get a complete picture, have students set forth specific categories before contrasting the two countries (Esslin presents his data in "block method"; having students identify points asks them to restructure the information in their own minds). Categories to consider include the following:

> early history/approach/effects
>
> present advantages/present disadvantages
>
> future solutions/requirements

Esslin begins this piece with the one invention that characterizes the onset of "modern humanity"—the printing press. His tone is formal, yet accessible; the sentences are complex, for the most part, and written in the third person. The last paragraph differs in several respects. First of all, students may sense a feeling of immediacy as he begins this paragraph with an "And." Second, and more apparent to most students, Esslin uses the first person in addressing his readers. The shift is obvious. As a writer, he has moved closer to his readers. His purpose, thus, moves from that of informing to that of persuading.

In his closing arguments, Esslin uses ethical appeals at every opportunity. Ask students to list, from paragraph 25 until the end, the words that are loaded with ethical connotations (doing this in groups may speed up the process here). Students should recognize, among other possibilities, the following list of power-packed choices: "solution," "parochialism," "enlightened," "responsible," "sensibility," "resources," "talents," "respectability," "superior," "first-rate," "well-being," "national tragedy," "dispirited complacency," "democracy," "deficiency," "dangers," "depressing," "false," "horrifying," "slavery," "civil rights," "segregation," "will," "determination," "wise."

Not only does Esslin write passionately by the end of his argument, but, as a fair-minded person, he also considers his opposition's positions. He acknowledges the strengths of American television (par. 15), as well as the problems inherent in operating in such a large area as America (par. 18). Has he acknowledged enough? Students may want to consider whether Esslin has, perhaps, overlooked any other differences between the two countries in drawing his conclusions.

An obvious connection between television and American society is, of course, the preoccupation with commercialism at the expense of art. Students may come up with other connections as well, such as the preference for entertainment over education; the preference for fantasy over reality; the connection between paternalism and male-female relationships in America; the sense of competition as opposed to cooperation. Whether or not these reflections are justified should be up for discussion.

Finally, students are asked to close the text for a while and turn on their televisions. With the advent of cable television, Americans have a variety of networks available to them. Perhaps assigning specific stations to groups of students will make for a more fair-minded study. However, remind students that even when they watch a station concerned primarily with the news (or sports or health, or whatever), they still have to look for the entertainment factor. Is the primary purpose of the program to inform or educate, or is it still mainly to entertain? Remind students to take careful, observational notes while watching their assigned network.

In rebuttal to Esslin, students may wish to write an argument that upholds the importance of television as an entertainment industry. Further, they can also compare American network sitcoms with the programs on their PBS station. Finally, they can write (and present) their own opinions on the importance of either public television or private networking.

Lester C. Thurow, U.S. Drug Policy: Colossal Ignorance (p. 581)
(Cross-Chapter Connections: "Rights and Responsibilities")

In recent years, the United States has become increasingly concerned with illegal drug use and sales. The problems, as seen by many, cross borders from race to race, class to class, age to age. In discussing this topic, allow students to bring in their own experiences and observations. How bad is the drug problem in this country? What possible solutions could students in the class offer to relieve this problem?

In a clear and direct manner, the author reveals his own solutions to this problem. From the first paragraph alone, students may see that the author is not only direct, but learned as well. In this case, a reader may very well feel like a student in a lecture hall instead of a co-pilot on this journey. Students should recognize that authors' tones and approaches differ, and the importance in writing is to match the style with the idea. Thurow uses a direct, authoritative tone to suggest the urgency of his topic and to press for consideration of what he knows will be an unpopular point of view.

Basically, Thurow is saying that the border approach to controlling the flow of illegal drugs has and will continue to fail. Therefore, the war on drugs should be fought in America. As he says, the focus should be on the "user, not the supplier" (par. 14). To support this idea, Thurow compares foreign crop growers to America's tobacco growers. The analogy goes something like this: Both groups are in a business to make money, and in many ways, the business of the country depends on this produce, as well. What country has the right to tell another culture what not to grow?

The tobacco analogy is just one of the points Thurow makes with which he hopes his audience will identify. He approaches his stance from other directions as well. He points to the demand curve (economics), he points to the temptation of American officials (human nature), and he points to the era of Prohibition of alcohol (history). Although students may disagree as to which argument is most effective, this essay serves as a model for the many ways in which an argument can be developed. Thurow appeals to common sense, ethics, logic, and emotions.

After examining the "colossal ignorance" of America's present attack on drugs for almost the entire article, in his last three paragraphs, Thurow comes to his solution. The three ways to focus on the user fall under the following categories: education, incarceration, and social changes. Thurow does admit the one drawback to this solution: It would be expensive. Students should go further and discuss whether or not any of these three means to his end are probable or possible, as well. In groups, students should also brainstorm to see if they can come up with any other solutions or to see if they can provide some practical details for any one of the author's ideas.

In deciding whether they would vote for such a man if he were running for office, students should note how their initial impressions of the man versus their evaluation of his ideas play into this decision.

How does his character come across in this piece? Does he seem fair-minded? Does he seem intelligent? Experienced? What other traits might they look for in a person running for office?

Students who desire to work more with this topic are invited to write their own rebuttal to this argument or to research another author's views on this subject.

Mustafa Nabil, The Arab's Image (p. 584)
(Cross-Chapter Connections: "Ways of Learning," "Rights and Responsibilities")

In this selection, the author describes the narrow, stereotyped image many Americans have of Arabs. In their prereading journals, students may come up with the same stereotypical symbols that Nabil describes in this piece: harems, camels, oil magnates, bedouin lifestyles, flowing robes, gold, wine.

If you choose to have the class discuss their impressions before reading this piece, you may want to ask them where they got these impressions. Was it from someone they know? From a book? Television? Movies? Students should aim to be as specific as possible in these answers.

If students compare the first sentence of this piece with other opening lines in the selections in Section 4, "Writing to Persuade," they will find the author's proposed action right up front rather than coming toward the end of the argument. Writers have countless options at their disposal, and students should consider why this author chose such a direct approach. Stepping back a minute, you may even want students to read just the first line and then write a quick, honest reaction. By comparing responses, the class will be able to witness the effect this one line has had on the class as a whole.

If students have not done the prereading exercises, they may have a tendency to be defensive when Nabil lists the general impressions Americans have. However, if students have completed this writing, all they have to do is look back to their initial reactions to see whether or not Nabil is probably right about the image many Americans have about Arabs. Still, some students may see Nabil's tone as a bit harsh. Based on the stereotyping he describes, does Nabil convince us of his right to declare a campaign against "American society at large"?

Further, readers should look closely at Nabil's supporting examples. Nabil lashes out at American television, but gives two examples: "Vegas" and "Hawaii Five-O" (both of which are out of prime-time spots and are reruns of old shows). Nabil accuses commercials of showing bloodthirsty Arabs but gives no example here. One cartoon is presented as an example of how newspapers stereotype Arabs. Lastly, movies are included in the list, yet the author offers no names of specific movie titles. Does Nabil need support in each of these cases? How much support? Should readers accept an argument as fact without support or examples? Students should become tuned in to statements that "beg the question" instead of stating facts or essential support.

Nabil's strongest argument may very well be the point that the typical portrayal of an Arab does not match with the real lives of Arab Americans. However, in order to make this argument valid, some students may recognize that the author needs to do more than blame American media and education. He needs to support these allegations in writing.

This piece reads like a call to action for a specific group of people. The author may have several purposes in mind. First, he may want to open people's eyes to ignorance of stereotyping. He is certainly right about this point. Second, he wants people to be more aware of the images that they get, secondhand, from the media. Third, he may be seeking support for action toward the media or education.

After reading and discussing Nabil's concerns, students are urged to become astute researchers of information in newspapers, on television and radio, and in ads. In addition, they may want to conduct their own survey (the prereading question they had would be a good start) to discover how students and faculty on campus view Arab-Americans. In addition, students can watch for media stereotyping of other groups of people: teenagers, senior citizens, blacks, women, Asians, short people, heavy people, and so on.

Paul Fusell, Should Hiroshima Have Been Bombed? (p. 587)
(Cross-Chapter Connections: "Ways of Learning," "Roots and Memories," "Rights and Responsibilities")

Students have two particularly challenging prereading choices before them. With time and distance, can we ever see clearly a difficult situation in which we had to make a decision? Do we lose our defensive nature? Do we understand more now? In addition to this, students can thrash the old adage, "All is fair in love and war." Should love and war be set aside with this special privilege?

Once students have thought about the past and questioned the wisdom of the present, they are ready to listen to Paul Fussell's argument that yes, considering conditions of the world and the war at the time, Hiroshima should have been bombed. Besides historical events, Fussell bases much of his analysis on his own experience as a soldier. As he writes in his lambasting of Galbraith, "experience is crucial in this case" (par. 2). Students may be divided on this issue. Certainly, Fussell had been in combat before. However, if he had been in Japan, if he had witnessed firsthand the destruction, would his ideas be the same?

Actually, if one were to characterize Fussell's reaction to those who disagree with the bombing, one would have to say he seems simply fed up. He does not see the decision as one that involved ethics. He sees it as a practical move in a difficult situation, much along the lines of a chess game. Someone had to win, and someone had to lose. As he writes in his final argument, "Coarse self-interest is the rule" (par. 13).

To further explain the uniqueness of wartime situations, Fussell provides the reader with graphic details and quotes from fellow soldiers. As a result, Fussell accomplishes several things. First of all, he pulls the readers into the realities of war, away from the ivory tower theorists. Second, he shows how both sides were injured, how war doesn't discriminate between men, women, children, or race. Third, he also sets himself apart from the soldiers who were vulgar and crude. In a way, he is saying, "See? I am not like them. My reasons for feeling the way I do about the bomb are reasons based on logic—not emotion or prejudice."

Besides showing the thinking and beliefs on both sides of this issue, Fussell is a master when it comes to word choice. No matter what paragraph students choose to analyze, they will find a persuasive richness, especially in his choices of verbs and phrase modifiers. Not only that, but the title of his piece is also carefully crafted. Note the difference between "Should Hiroshima Have Been Bombed?" (a question in the passive voice, without mention of a country) and "Should the United States (or We) Have Bombed Hiroshima?" (The second title implies direct action and focuses on the doer, as well as the action.)

Fussell's last—and probably strongest—argument comes in the final paragraph when he explains what life is like in combat. Soldiers, he writes, cannot be expected to be "sensitive humanitarians." Those who understand would want war stopped, no matter what the means. Some students may accept this argument, while others may see a breakdown between comparing hand-to-hand combat with the dropping of the atom bomb. In the first action, a split-second decision has to be made; in the second scenario, there is time to discuss and weigh out the pros and cons of such a decision.

Overall, although Fussell's word choices are full of emotional appeal, the author takes a reasonable, logical, practical course in this argument. As stated in the beginning, he assumes an authoritative air based on his initial belief that experience wins out over theory. Considering his position, this is probably the best choice of appeals he could make. After all, he claims, this isn't a humanitarian, ethical question, really. If he expresses any emotion, it borders on anger and impatience. To him, the issue is clear. He wastes little time showing the reader what he himself sees.

As far as making a connection to this essay, perhaps the more interesting Extended Thinking suggestion is that of interviewing other veterans who were, like Fussell, in World War II. What does experience teach us about war? To answer this question, Fussell's essay is only a start; the real answer remains to be seen in what students discover for themselves through a primary means of gaining knowledge: the interview.

Michael Walzer, Hiroshima: An Act of Terrorism (p. 596)
(Cross-Chapter Connections: "Rights and Responsibilities," "American Dreams and Creations")

For students to connect to both sides of the bombing of Hiroshima, they should read Paul Fussell's essay (text p. 587) before Walzer's argument. From the onset, Walzer makes it clear that he is writing this piece as a response to Fussell's initial argument. He feels that, overall, Fussell comes across as a macho soldier who believes that America went to Japan, showed them who was boss, and came home, victorious and proud. Is this the image that students have after reading Fussell? If students say yes, he did come across as a boaster to them, then they should be prepared to say why they feel that way by specific reference to the text. Those who feel Fussell uses his experience to support his point may be right. However, students might want to discuss the difference between being proud and being boastful.

In addition, students should stop and think about Walzer's paraphrase of Fussell's main point. Is it adequate? Is it fair? Overall, most students will agree that, although Fussell may not word his primary argument exactly the way Walzer does, the general idea is accurate. War in itself is a crime, and, therefore, whatever can be done to end it must be done.

In direct contrast to Fussell's view that decisions in war are not bound to ethics, Walzer claims that "bombing Hiroshima was an act of terrorism." It was, in this author's mind, a deliberate choice that moved war beyond the battlefield and into Japanese homes, schools, and businesses. Such an act was like a terrorist attack, according to Walzer, because the intent was to scare the Japanese leaders into surrender. You may want to ask students if this analogy holds up in relation to purpose and leadership.

To reach his conclusion, Fussell draws from various sources. In addition, he draws on his own experiences as a soldier. In his mind, this experience has given him more insights as to what war is like than it has to "outsiders" who merely write and think about war. At this point, you may ask students to share the journal entries they wrote before reading this essay. Does distance give one perspective on the past, or does our involvement in the past cause us to hold tight to the decisions we made at the time? The question remains: Does Fussell's experience enlighten or blind him to the implications of this event?

In Walzer's case, he calls not on experience but, instead, refers to literature, history, situation ethics, and logic. Mostly though, at the end, he raises the ethical question: Aren't all men responsible for some sense of moral order? He raises the question and leaves it unanswered; his rhetoric here is clear. His argument is passionate, and his appeal is ethical. However, while Fussell may depend too much on his experience to provide truth, Walzer may make theoretical statements without finding adequate historical or experiential support. Students' preferences will certainly be divided in this case.

While Walzer upholds ideals and Fussell draws on experience, students are urged to find other sources that deal with this same issue. What other factors may come into play here? Can they find an author who offers new information? In addition, students may find contradictions among authors concerning the facts and events surrounding crucial events in World War II. Fussell would say these events matter; Walzer would say no matter what the facts, the end in this case didn't justify the means.

Robert Olen Butler, The Trip Back (p. 600)
(Cross-Chapter Connections: "Arriving," "Roots and Memories," "Parents and Children," "Men and Women")

In this selection, students will find themselves crossing borders between men and women, young and old, American images and Asian memories, and, among other things, the ways in which the past and present affect our futures. To prepare for the richness of this fictional piece, students should take time to write about the memories in their lives they hope never to lose. They should also pause and think about what life might be like when they're older, as well as the things in their lives they value now.

The title of this piece is simple, in the syntactical sense. However, it has several levels of meanings that students might recognize. Students might initially connect it to the old grandfather's trip to America—a trip back to his family. However, coming back implies a sort of leaving. He hasn't really left his family, has he? More aptly, the title might refer to his trip back to his past. Thus, the "trip" has little to do with planes and new places; it has to do with the past he longs for once again.

Another twist on the title involves the speaker and his wife. At the end of this piece, they, too, have made an important trip back to each other. On this same note, the speaker has made an individual trip back to his past as well. He has, in the final paragraph, remembered his roots when he feels in the depths of his memory "a breeze off the South China Sea."

As Khanh drives to the airport, his mind rehearses the details of small businesses that are scattered by the highway. The first group can be categorized as those of common laborers; others capitalize on the simple things they have at hand: food, spare parts, old things. The next three places reflect hobbies of this region: drinking, fishing, sporting.

And finally, there are the luxuries for this area: doughnuts and dreams of making it. Obviously, this area is poor, disconnected from the American city, disconnected from the American dream of money, power, and success.

Before answering Question No. 3, students should think about their images of a business person as compared to their images of a poet. Certainly, the first occupation is, to most people, an acceptable position, one in which a person has a chance to climb the ladder, be successful. A poet, on the other hand, is what? A dreamer? An idealist? One removed from society's inner circles? By beginning this way, what impression does Khanh give to his readers? Is he, by the way, telling the truth? You may want to direct students to the fine details Khanh includes throughout this piece. Does he see life through the eyes of a businessman, a poet, something else? (A combination, perhaps, is the truest answer. This also fits nicely with the fact that he is a combination of America and Asia as well.)

Again, by stating outright that he is a businessman, Khanh sounds a note of mainstream America. He seems deeply concerned with being American, although he does talk about the honor in which Vietnamese hold their families. He still has a shrine in his home, although he is quick to add that this is for the Catholic saints. Again, he seems to need to make sure he is viewed as an all-out American.

However, the major difference between Khanh and his wife, Mai, lies in the fact that Mai is more open to expressing her feelings, to embracing her Vietnamese culture, while Khanh remembers the rituals but has separated himself, at least emotionally, from his culture's past. As he says, "I found that I was no longer comfortable with the old ways. Like the extended family. Like other things, too. . . . I was a good American now" (par. 17). Also, Khanh appears concerned with who he appears to be, as he begs the reader, "Do not misjudge me. I am not a cold man" (par. 9).

After Khanh realizes that Mr. Chinh does not remember his granddaughter, he is scared. He doesn't explain why. He simply says he was concerned for himself at this point. But what's the impression that students have of the grandfather? He is an old man, with glasses, in a checked suit coat, an old man who has come a long way, an old man who talks of cars, and smiles. Would students find him frightening? Can they offer reasons why Khanh feels afraid? (Khanh says it isn't because he's afraid of growing old. What else might it be, then?)

As stated earlier, this piece is rich in symbolism, rich in borders. Useless businesses border the superhighway; the "Lost and Old Rivers" border the islands; Mr. Khanh borders on being a poet; in bed, initially, the wife and husband border one another, but they do not merge; Khanh's feelings border on tenderness, but he can't get over his image of what it means to be an American; Mr. Chinh borders on the present, but his mind is more comfortable in the past; as an American, Khanh borders on losing his culture; although Mai is Chinh's granddaughter, he will more or less be her boarder, her role will be that of innkeeper.

Besides delving into the borders and symbols of this story, students may wish to go outside of this piece and listen to the memories and experiences of older people they know or would like to know. Such conversations—possibly in the form of interviews—move them, literally, beyond their own borders and encourage them to reach out to someone else's territory.

Denise Levertov, What Were They Like? (p. 611)
(Cross-Chapter Connections: "Roots and Memories," "Ways of Learning")

Like Robert Olen Butler's story (text p. 600), this poem deals with the memories of a country before a war and the realities of this same country, Vietnam, years later. In contrast to "The Trip Back," however, the speaker in this poem realizes that, given time, memories, too, fade out until an entire civilization's gifts and influences may disappear.

Ask students to write a description of who they think the speaker in this poem is. Some may see a young, wide-eyed child. Others may see a school-aged child, one who is trying to piece together a history lesson of sorts. Or perhaps they see a young assistant working with an anthropologist or a historian. Whatever they picture, students should realize that the speaker asks questions that move beyond the obvious and into the heart of a culture: What did these people do for light? How did they celebrate spring? What were their habits? Were they noisy? Quiet? Did they laugh? Were they a serious people? What did they do with the precious materials of their land? Were they simple people or did they like decorations? Is there a piece of literature that reveals their myths and mysteries, their hopes and dreams? Were they orators or harmonizers?

Clearly, these answers can be found only by asking the people themselves, by listening to the stories and the myths that formed this culture. History books may tell the facts and figures. This speaker wants to know the soul of this culture as well.

And who is answering the questions? Although several answers are possible, the person either was very young at the time ("It is not remembered") or is at least a generation removed from the experience of Vietnam. Another possibility, and perhaps the best guess considering the language the responder uses ("When peaceful clouds were reflected in the paddies/and the water buffalo stepped surely along terraces"), is that the responder is a very old person from Vietnam. Some things are remembered. Others are not. The responder, perhaps, is like Mr. Chinh ("The Trip Back," text p. 600).

The final metaphor in this piece, that of the moths in moonlight, reveals the fragile nature of a species, while at the same time alluding to the lightness and wholeness of the Vietnamese culture and landscape. The singing, like moths, might be notes fluttering in the air, rising high into the sky. The singing, seen in this light, sounds more like delicate wind chimes—ethereal and in harmony with the night.

The connection between moths and the people of Vietnam is, of course, the short life span, the speed with which the fluttering was stopped. In addition, one may not think that the extinction of a moth means much—except, as Levertov shows us, once it's gone, we can never hold it or know it again. In the final line, all is quiet. As Levertov writes, "It is silent now." The "It" here can stand for several images: the singing, the screams, the echo, the laughter, the noise of a culture, the culture itself.